"New Haven Family
The Lenders

Bagels! Bagels!
and more Bagels!

Library of Congress Catalog Card Number: 79-5237
Copyright © 1979 by Rand McNally & Company
All rights reserved.
Printed in the United States of America.

Illustrator, Bonnie Gates
Designer, Kirk George Panikis
Editor, Dorothy L. Millikan

Bagels! Bagels! and more Bagels!

A Saga of Good Eating with Recipes, Legend and Lore

by Nao Hauser and Sue Spitler

RAND McNALLY & COMPANY

Chicago • New York • San Francisco

CONTENTS

FOREWORD

As a teen-ager during the mid-1940s, I shared an attic bedroom in a two-family house with my brother Marvin, who is ten years younger than I. The family bagel bakery was in the backyard, which made it rather easy for brother Sam, ten years my senior, to wake me when one of the two bakers we employed had " over-shnapsed" himself and not shown up for work. After filling in, I would return to bed for a few winks before going to school. Marvin was a light sleeper and his bed was only a few feet away from mine. Half asleep he would peer over at me, and I would jokingly ask the same dumb question, "What do you want to be when you grow up?" Whether groggy or wide awake, Marvin invariably would answer "A bagel baker." Marvin was really saying that he wanted to be just like his father.

Harry Lender learned to bake bagels in the old country but he never allowed us to forget that it was here in the New World that he was able to practice his craft and grow. He spent an enormous number of hours working in the bakery. At the same time, he encouraged his kids to seek "a better life" on the outside. Obviously, however, our father's warmth, love and dedication to family and business made a far greater impression on us than his urgings that we leave the "world of bageling."

Ours was one of a handful of bagel bakeries outside New York City. We baked about 200 dozen bagels a day for delis and grocers. If all the Jewish folk in New Haven simultaneously had lost their taste for lox, the Lenders would have been out looking for work the next day.

Today, 17 years after we introduced our first frozen roundie, a real live bagel boom is in full swing. Most good-sized cities have retail bakeries, and just about every supermarket in the nation has a Lender's frozen bagel department. Jewish customers have discovered that the bagel is a lot more versatile than the traditional breakfast of bagels and smoked salmon would imply. Non-Jewish consumers have made a more dramatic discovery: the product itself. Of the more than a million bagels our company produces each day, over 80 percent are enjoyed in non-Jewish homes.

What has all this meant to the Lenders? Sam is chairman of the board of our still family-owned business, which now employs more than 300 people. Marvin is executive vice president and the current inheritor of the early morning emergency calls. Now when they come, however, it is not because one of our employees has imbibed a bit too much and had a "power failure"; it is more likely that one of our four plants has had the latter difficulty.

As president of the company, I have by-passed receiving the emergency call and instead get opportunities to chat with talented writers and editors who feel strongly enough to write a book dedicated solely to the crusty little devil's usage, history and charm. *Bagels! Bagels! and more Bagels!* is a cookbook and then some. It is educational. It is fun. And its timing couldn't be better, for in 1980 we will celebrate the fiftieth anniversary of the frozen food industry. It was in Springfield, Massachusetts, on March 6, 1930, that the world's first frozen food department was born. A multitude of ethnic foods have found their way into the national "melting pot" through this American-created technique of food preservation and distribution. Bagels, of course, have joined them in freezer cases everywhere—demonstrating vividly that the land of opportunity remains just that!

Who could have imagined that bagels, a bagel bakery or a bagel-baking family would make such dramatic strides! If Harry Lender were alive, he would echo words said many times before and still pertinent today . . . "only in America!"

Murray Lender

BAGELS AS A WAY OF LIFE

Bagels can solve a lot of problems. Like what to serve for breakfast, brunch, lunch and dinner. And what to have on hand for friendly interlopers who lope in from time to time. And how to please your nephew Larry who won't eat meat, fish or anything pink. And how to pacify your best friend Trudy who thinks you're stuck in a meatloaf rut. And what to take to the movies when you can't get a date. And what you can turn to when your heart aches and the phone doesn't ring.

You might even consider bagels the last of the all-round lovers. With a bagel you know you've found a meaningful relationship from the very first bite. A bagel never acts coy or blasé. On the contrary, it grips your teeth in a passionate embrace every time you meet. Not just a peck on the incisors, but a full-scale tug of the jaws. The dense, crusty ring cares enough to engage you in its chewiness, to lavish you with flavor.

That's why we have come to devote a book to the subject of bagels. We wanted to record all the good times we've had with the robust rings. The moments of chewy bliss, the joys of daily encounters. The mornings of cozy comfort, the evenings of surprise entertainment. All the sandwiches, casseroles, salads and desserts we've enjoyed thanks to bagels. All the gravies they've thickened, the fondues they've dipped, the crumb crusts they've held together. In short, we owe a lot of great meals to bagels and we wanted to acknowledge our debt.

In *Bagels! Bagels! and more Bagels!* you'll find over 150 recipes and serving suggestions. If you've never considered bagels as anything more than vehicles for cream cheese and lox, you'll be amazed by their versatility. For us, however, bagels have never been a casual Sunday-morning affair. We've lived with bagels long enough to appreciate their stalwart contributions to all kinds of dishes. Their staunch resistance to sogginess and dissolution in all culinary combinations has won our deepest admiration. Their day-in and day-out dependability has won our heartfelt loyalty. Indeed, bite by bite, recipe by recipe, we've come to regard bagels as a way of life.

Ours is what you might call an "open relationship." It is open to every culture and cuisine—French, Italian, Greek, Mexican, Swiss, Hawaiian and Chinese, to name only a few. Although the bagel came to this country in the skillful hands of Jewish bagel bakers, success has made it accessible to all kinds of cookery. Therefore, the recipes in this book do not conform exclusively to Jewish dietary laws. The bagel itself, however, remains strictly kosher. So most of the non-kosher recipes can be adapted by changing one or two of the other ingredients and using kosher dairy substitutes. People who adhere to vegetarian or low-calorie diets will find separate chapters full of such fare—they're natural showcases for the bagel's simple, cholesterol-free charms.

Bagels are by nature generous and well-rounded. Their chubby contours are usually split horizontally to provide two eminently toastable, spreadable rings. The recipes in this book assume that the bagels have been cut in this way; so when we say "Place bagel under broiler" or "Spread on Bagel," we always mean bagel halves.

You'll notice that next to the bagel quantity in many of the recipes there is a parenthetical reference to "pumpernickel," "rye," "raisin 'n honey" or one of the other bagel flavors. This is not a secret code; it's just a way of suggesting that you might like to substitute the flavor indicated for a plain bagel in the recipe. Of course, every meaningful relationship is open to creative change. So feel free to experiment with various kinds of bagels. You'll find them studded with raisins; sweetened with honey; accented with onion, garlic, poppy seeds or sesame seeds; and enriched with eggs or rye or whole wheat flour.

Some people are known by the bagels they eat and you'll meet them throughout this book. These are people like our neighbor Madeleine who, with her discerning sense of delicacy, always chooses half-size bagelettes. And our buddy George, who gets all his gusto from pumpernickel rounds. And Lorraine, whose quest for a husband led to a raisin 'n honey romance. For these and all of our other friends, bagels have met the complex demands of diverse tastes and appetites.

For us, one bagel has simply led to another . . . and another. And so we find ourselves following a round, glossy path in the everyday pursuit of pleasure!

A HISTORY FULL OF HOLES

We wish we could present a heroic saga of bagel history. A drum and bagel corps, perhaps, rolling over the forces of white bread. Or a team of bagel-nauts hurtling through space to land on a cream cheese moon. Or even a frontier bagel brigade rounding up crumb-trailing outlaws.

Glory, in short, is what we envisioned for the bagel's genealogy. But the facts, scant as they are, refuse to bear us out. So we will present the contents of the bagel archives strictly as we found them, in a series of mouth-watering, if not quite epic, tales.

A Bagel Has No Beginning

We have no idea where bagels came from. There is no inventor whose name and visage we can enshrine in a Bagel Hall of Fame. But, appropriately enough, the first written reference to bagels concerns their association with birth.

The year is 1610; the place, Cracow, Poland. The event seems rather extraordinary to us: The town legislators have passed a decree outlawing the giving of bagels as gifts except "to midwives and the women present when a pregnant woman gives birth."

Why this rigid proscription? Because bagels were thought to have magical powers. It's strange but true! The good citizens of Cracow, like those of many other Eastern European towns, placed their faith in bagels. Because the lawmakers did not want people to treat lightly the bagel's alleged ability to ward off evil demons, they reserved the gift of bagels for life's most critical hours.

A Bagel Has No End

> "People fast the Ninth of Ab . . .
> People eat bagels with ash before the fast."
> —Folksong from Vitebsk province

> "The fast of the Ninth of Ab is observed after a milk meal which includes a bagel—a crusty doughnut-shaped bun—or an egg dipped in ashes."
> *Encyclopedia Judaica*

The Ninth of Ab is a day of great sorrow on the Jewish calendar; observance of a fast on this date commemorates the destruction of the ancient Temple in Jerusalem. How did it come about that the same ring-shaped amulet reserved for births should reappear in a ritual of mourning? It was all part of the magic of bagels. Because of their circular form, bagels came to symbolize the continuous cycle of life—without beginning and end.

The Power of Bagels

Lest you be foolish enough to doubt the power of bagels, we offer this testimony from the record of the great 18th-century rabbi and mystical teacher, Israel Baal Shem Tov:

One day the Baal Shem Tov tried to impress upon a simpleton the value of a bagel. Even the non-Jews who worked with him in the fields would come to the fool's aid, the rabbi explained, if he summoned them by tossing a bagel. Soon after, this wisdom was borne out when the simpleton fell into a river. Struggling against the current and fearing that he would drown, the fool despaired of being rescued. He could see people on a mountaintop in the distance. But how could he alert them to his plight? Then he remembered the bagel he carried in his pocket. So he grasped the water-logged ring and threw it as hard as he could in the direction of the mountain. And sure enough, the people saw him and came to save him, with God's help.

To Thine Own Bagels Be True

Ah, at last a bit of romance! Or at least that's what we thought when we came upon another report of the Baal Shem Tov's great wisdom. But we'll let you judge the record for yourself:

A young girl was engaged to marry an important man. Her future held the promise of high social status and commensurate wealth. Yet her dreams of happiness lay elsewhere. The Baal Shem Tov stepped in to save her from apostasy. "This engagement should be broken off," the rabbi declared, "because you are unworthy of marrying an important man when you know that you only want to marry a baker and sit in the market with bagels."

The Value of Bagels

The distressing circumstances of the young girl forced to choose between social position and bagels should not leave you with the impression that the glossy rings did not offer a little glitter of their own.

A collection of old Jewish proverbs published in Warsaw in 1908 provides some clues to the historical market value of bagels.

One proverb punningly proclaims: "Eating bagels leaves a hole in your pocket."

And another hints at the fact that bagels were considered important enough to be subject to commercial regulation with this analogy: "It's like a bagel for a groschen." In other words, bagels carried a fixed price. So if you were to meet the baker's wife in the marketplace with her wares stacked like quoits on a long stick, you couldn't haggle for a bargain. The bagel vendor's job was by no means glamorous, but it had a certain dignity because bagels were much in demand.

"We Must Buy Bagels . . ."

One reason bagel sales were brisk in every village marketplace throughout Eastern Europe was that people continued to believe that the rings would bring good luck. Indeed, a 19th-century Yiddish folksong from Russia linked the spell of bagels to the joys of marriage:

> "We must buy bagels
> And spead them with butter,
> Father and Mother
> Should lead you to the *huppah* (wedding canopy)."

Baking Bagels for a Whole Year

In the 20th century, the superstitions surrounding bagels yielded to a specific dream of freedom from poverty and persecution—recorded here in a turn-of-the-century Lithuanian folksong:

> "I your groom and you my bride,
> We are both an equal pair.
> In America we can bake bagels
> For a whole year."

11

Acting on this tender sentiment, thousands of Eastern European Jews gathered their meager resources and booked passage to America. We would like to think that the stars continued to shine in the newlyweds' eyes and that they found bagel bliss on these shores. But this is not a sentimental record. If it were, we'd provide the immigrants with a better reception than the one they met with in the squalid tenements of New York City's Lower East Side. There the "equal pair" doubtless baked bagels for a whole year—often for 12 hours a day, six days a week, in a dimly lit and unventilated cellar bakery.

Bagels Get Organized

There's nothing we'd like better than to let the Old World violins fade into the distance at this point and strike up a rousing chorus of "There's No Business Like the Bagel Business!" We'd put bagels up in lights, give them a smashing Broadway debut, make them the talk of the town. . . .

But the facts won't allow it. Bagels made their American debut in rather a different fashion. For most of the first half of this century, they remained the province of immigrant bakers and the Sunday morning pride of Jewish households. They did, however, enter the mainstream in two ways—through humor and unionization.

In the best show biz tradition, bagels acquired an "act" when immigrant connoisseurs teamed them with cream cheese and lox. Taste, not humor, was the intent. But there was something comical about this odd-sounding trio of treats, this relatively humble homage highly regaled as the succulent symbol of New World prosperity. And Jewish comedians did not fail to serve up this bounty for laughs as often as possible. Thus bagels traded their magical aura for a kind of rollicking recognition—not the publicity we would have wished, perhaps, but effective all the same.

On the serious side, bagels made headlines through the efforts of the bagel bakers' union, which was first organized some 80 or 90 years ago. In Europe, many of the bakers had worked in fairly large commercial bakeries and their sophisticated skills were highly regarded. So, not surprisingly, they banded together in New York to improve the wages and miserable working conditions of the cellar bakeries.

Newspaper reports of organizing and strike activity go back as far as 1900. But it was not until 1951 that the union received the ultimate tribute to newsworthiness with this front-page headline in *The New York Times:* "Bagel Famine Threatens in City. Labor Dispute Puts Hole in Supply." The accompanying story about the strike of 300 bagel bakers decried the "bad news for addicts of the bagel" and estimated normal demand for the product at 100,000 dozen each weekend. The city responded to the crisis with classic ingenuity: A special mediator renowned for having settled a lox strike some years earlier was brought in to end the dispute.

During the interim days of dearth, "Shopkeepers and restaurant owners reported that substitutes such as toasted seeded rolls, Bialystock rolls, which have a depressed center sprinkled with onions, and egg bagels, a sweeter variety but not the McCoy, were being thrown into the bagel void with varying degrees of reception."

Somehow New York City's recent crises seem to pale by comparison!

A Sign of the Times

As America entered the 1900s, the lawyer for the Bagel Bakers Council of Greater New York heralded a new era in bagel relations. Elaborating on his claim that bagels had been finding many non-Jewish friends, the official boasted to a *New York Times* reporter that "Last St. Patrick's Day we turned out green-dyed bagels for Irish bagelniks and their sympathizers."

Bagels See the Light

One of the most heartwarming moments in bagel history came in October, 1963, when *The New York Times* recorded this blessed event:

Bagel Bakers See the Light
And Retail Business Blossoms

The crusty bagel, which made good in New York after a perilous journey from Russia and Poland around the turn of the century, has gone places again. Specifically, up.

At first, nearly every bagel bakery in the city set up shop in a steamy, dank and poorly lighted basement.

The basements are still gloomy, but the old brick hearth ovens have been discarded and everybody has moved to ground level, where shiny stainless steel ovens now reflect sunlight.

Explaining the exodus yesterday, Health Department officials said it all started when a couple of bakery owners, spurred by department complaints about unsanitary conditions, abandoned their "dungeons" for street-level quarters. . . .

They put up colored neon signs that blinked "Hot Bagels" far into the night. Sunday brunch lovers quickly got the message.

The retail idea spread, and today, all 26 bagel bakeries in the city are on ground level and the public is welcome.

All concerned are happy that the good old days are gone—the Health Department, which now has few problems with the bakeries; the owners, who sell about 2,000,000 bagels a week; and the union bakers, whose deft hands give life to the plain roll with the hole in the middle.

Oh, Pioneers!

Every American saga, it seems, must have its westward trek. And so we next encounter bagels blazing a trail across the continent.

They rode neither horses nor Conestoga wagons. Instead, they galloped off in freezer trucks loaded at Lender's Bagel Bakery in Connecticut—in a revolutionary departure for bagels!

Until the mid-1960s, bagels resided mainly in East Coast cities. Their mobility was severely circumscribed by their notorious tendency to go stale within 24 hours. And their numbers were limited by the production capacity of the highly skilled bagel bakers. How, then, could they expand their horizons and win the heart of a vast, widespread nation?

Well, it took modern technology and Yankee ingenuity to come up with a series of answers. In 1962 Lender's made the first great breakthrough when they discovered that the fresh, chewy rings could be frozen without any damage to flavor or texture.

Once they were frozen, the bagels could be shipped across country and distributed through supermarkets. Which meant that the market for bagels could be expanded indefinitely. Which, in turn, meant that the Lender family could no longer meet the demand for bagels with traditional shaping and baking techniques. So they helped make the first bagel-shaping machines operational and installed them in automated production lines.

By 1964, Lender's had achieved their current status as the largest bagel bakery in the country. Today, they employ 300 people and produce 1000 dozen bagels an hour on each of their five fully automated lines.

Success American-Style

Freezing changed the entire context of bagel chomping in America. The roundies rolled cross-country and entered supermarket freezer cases everywhere. Curious shoppers from Maine to California fell prey to the blandishments of the bagel's chubby charm. And familiarity with bagels bred hundreds of thousands of round-the-clock romances. Hungry for the bagel's cheery chewiness, bageleaters arranged daily breakfast meetings, lunchtime reunions and dinner-hour rendezvous.

A *New York Times* food writer summed up this state of affairs in 1969: "The bagel business isn't what it used to be. It's better. . . . In fact, it's booming. A lot of people who, just a few years ago, couldn't have told a bagel from lox, are eating the crusty, ring-shaped rolls with as much relish as did yesterday's Jewish immigrants on the Lower East Side."

Bagel Noshes and Other Nooks

Nowadays, many people like to carry on their love affairs in public. You'll often see them chewing shamelessly in full view of drooling bystanders. They hang out in eateries with funny names like "Bagel Nosh," "Barnum and Bagel," "H. Lender & Sons," "Bagels Plus" and even, or so we've been told, "The Existentialist Bagel Shop." These nationwide pleasure palaces cater to bagel cravings that may arise away from home. They usually serve all kinds of sandwiches, salads, soups and other foods—but only one kind of bread. We salute their "holesome" outlook!

"To Bagelville and Beyond"

We don't want you to think that bagels lapsed into crass materialism when business began to boom. Far from it! Do we find bagels lounging around country club swimming pools and smoking big, fat cigars? Not at all. Instead, we find them engaged in a fascinating exchange of ideas in the intellectual pages of *Saturday Review*.

Bagels first took to this literary circuit when the magazine published a travel article in 1964 titled "To Bagelville and Beyond." The author, treating his subject rather lightly throughout, made the mistake of tossing an unsubstantiated bagel tale to the letter-writing wolves. It was an understandable error. He was simply repeating an oft-circulated version of bagel history that claims the rings were invented in 1683 to honor John Sobieski, the Polish king who saved Vienna from Turkish invaders.

The story sounded harmless enough when it appeared. But the outcry against it reverberated for months afterward. Everyone and his bagel-baking uncle, it seems, had another chronology to offer. They traced bagels to ancient Egypt, Greece, Rome, India, China and the Neanderthal caves.

Only some twelve issues after the initial discourse on bagels had appeared did the controversy come to an end. Not with a bang, but with one last scholarly whimper: "I assure you that I, and thousands of readers like me," the letter-writer sniffed, "have not made up our minds about the question [of the bagel's origins]."

History Goes 'Round and 'Round . . .

If you seek to draw a lesson from the foregoing history, there are many from which to choose. Like "Never Underestimate the Power of a Bagel" or "Be True to Bagels and They'll Be True to You."

But we haven't given up our Hollywood dreams of bagel glory. Now what we'd really like for the next go-around is brilliant technicolor, gleaming regalia, footmen, horses, lights, action and, as the orchestra swells with the clamor of the 1812 Overture, we see Napoleon himself marshaling his troops for the Battle of Bageloo. . . .

BAGELS—BELIEVE IT OR NOT!

The following is a chronology of some of the great deeds, small accomplishments and quirks of fate that have helped to make bagels a household word.

May 31, 1946

According to *The New York Times,* an indignant Bronx housewife sent a bagel to each of three top Washington officials with notes warning that "this is what bread will look like" if the government were to permit bakers to reduce further the size of the standard loaf. The letter writer described a bagel as a mere "hole with a roll around it"—which may explain why she wasted perfectly good bagels on unexemplary politicians.

1955

Gertrude Berg, the actress, introduced a recipe for bagels in her book, *The Molly Goldberg Jewish Cookbook,* with this profound insight into the intrinsic sociability of the food: "The bagel is a lonely roll to eat all by yourself because in order for the true taste to come out you need your family. One to cut the bagels, one to toast them, one to put on the cream cheese and the lox, one to put them on the table, and one to supervise."

February 4, 1956

Reporting the settlement of yet another bagel bakers' strike, *The New York Times* proclaimed that "The bagel, a form of Jewish baked goods sometimes described as a doughnut with rigor mortis, will not disappear from New York tables." Proving once more that bagels will stick it out regardless of how they are slandered in the press.

November 3, 1962

The political strength of the bagel bakers' union came to light when a group of Long Island craftsmen refused to sully their product with onions imported from Bulgaria. "American onions, O.K.; Communist onions, no!" was the motto chanted by the dissident bagel bakers as they walked off the job. According to *The New York Times,* the union agent claimed "The men won't work if they have to put those onions on the bagels." Fortunately, the matter was resolved when the bakery owner agreed to return the offending onions to the supplier. We would hate to think of bagels embroiled in a Not-So-Cold War!

February 20, 1965

In a letter to *Saturday Review* magazine, a veteran of the Korean War recounted how six bagels sent by his mother had saved his life in the combat zone. It seems that the soldier had stuffed the gifts into his coat pockets, where they effectively deflected three enemy bullets. "The doctors said that only the adamantine hardness of the bagel could have resisted the force of the bullets," the grateful ex-G.I. recalled.

January 14, 1973

A neighborhood gang known as the "brotherhood of bagel people" came to light in a *New York Times* feature on a bagel bakery in Queens. The gang had always hung out on the street outside the bakery but its membership had changed over the years: "No longer is it a small coterie of middle-aged and elderly men from the slavic countries who produce bagels, but young men, whites and blacks, replete with Afro-hairdos, mustaches, beards and peace medals,who are the new rank and file." Which just goes to show that the faces may change, but a good cause will always be served (preferably with cream cheese)!

August 6, 1973

The famous food writer Mimi Sheraton announced in *New York* magazine that "a proper bagel is tough, firm, slightly doughy and should lie on your stomach for at least five hours after it has been consumed." We agree. There's nothing so frustrating as a three-hour bagel!

August 20, 1973

A perspicacious New York reader challenged Ms. Sheraton's bagel ideal by presenting *New York* magazine with this justification for a somewhat softer ring: ". . . if you try to bite into one side of a nice, solid crust, all your tuna fish comes squishing out the other. Softer bagels make your tuna fish manageable."

August 31, 1977

The opening of a bagel bakery in London was greeted in *The New York Times* with this memorable announcement: "The American bagel has rolled into London and is holed up in Edgewater Road." Londoners were over-whelmingly pleased with the novelty and business was booming, the article claimed. The shop owner added, "We haven't had anyone bring one back except an inebriated Englishman who thought they were supposed to have fillings." Which is the best recommendation for sobriety we've ever heard.

February 1, 1979

A Chicago *Sun-Times* food writer counseled bageleaters never to "use bagels in place of Frisbees." Nor to "replace snow tires with bagels"—a reference, perhaps, to that city's devastating '79 blizzard. The author also noted that an "estimated one billion bagels will be consumed this year and probably by people who have no interest in the roll's pedigree."

A BAGEL BAKER TELLS ALL!

Barry Bagelbaker is the one man in the bagel business who's seen it all, who's done it all, who's spent scores of years baking, studying and analyzing bagels. Indeed, he is a man whose very name is synonymous with the art. So when Mr. Bagelbaker agreed to grant *Bagels! Bagels! and more Bagels!* an exclusive interview, we hastened to his factory, where the following informative conversation took place:

BAGEL INQUIRERS: Tell us, Mr. Bagelbaker, how did you get started in the bagel business?

BARRY BAGELBAKER: I was kidnapped.

BI: Kidnapped?

BB: That's right. I was only a kid and my father was a bagel baker. And instead of letting me take a nap when I got home from school, he put me to work right away making bagels. So I was kidnapped.

BI: Can you tell us a little bit about how bagels were made in those days?

BB: A little bit? I could write a book! It wasn't easy. It took almost a whole night just to make the dough. Then, after we had mixed the dough—300 pounds of flour in that dough—and kneaded it like crazy, we would let it rise. After that, we would shape it into bagels.

BI: Did you have any special equipment?

BB: Yeah, I had very special hands. They worked like lightning. I'd take a piece of dough, roll it between my palms and then snap it into a ring around three fingers. I was so fast they used to call me "Buzzin' Barry," "Buzzin' " for short.

BI: How fast were you?

BB: I was so fast that all the girls would run away when they saw me coming. That's how fast I was!

BI: No, we mean how many bagels could you make?

BB: Oh that. A hundred, 150 dozen an hour.

BI: That must have been very hard on you—working all night.

BB: Terrible, terrible. But the worst thing was that I was losing money like crazy. It cost me a small fortune every night.

BI: Were the ingredients that expensive?

BB: Oh no. Flour, yeast, water, salt didn't cost that much. But I was losing my shirt at pinochle.

BI: Pinochle?

BB: Yeah. Every night me and the other bakers played pinochle. What else could we do while the bagels were rising?

BI: Well, it certainly seems like you've come a long way since then.

BB: Not long, round. We make everything round.

BI: Right. So tell us, how did you come around to this kind of factory?

BB: They made us do it

BI: "They"?

BB: That's right. They, the bageleaters of America. Once they caught on to bagels, there was no other way we could keep up with them.

BI: How do you keep up with them now?

BB: By baking 500,000 dozen bagels a week, freezing them and shipping them out immediately.

BI: That's a lot of bagels! How do you produce so many?

BB: Well, we start with a lot of flour—high-gluten, high-protein, unbleached flour. See those silos? Each one holds 100,000 pounds of flour. We go through a whole silo every three or four days.

BI: Where does it all go?

BB: It goes into a sifter. And then—and this I can hardly believe myself!—you just push a button and 400 pounds of flour falls—whoosh!—into the doughmixer, where we liven it up and leaven it with water, malt, sugar, yeast and salt. Then, if I want, I push another button—sometimes onions come out, sometimes poppy seeds, sesame seeds, garlic, raisins—whatever flavor I want. And nothing else—no artificial ingredients or preservatives. Then the doughmixer takes over—God bless it. Because I'll tell you one thing, if I had to mix all that dough by hand, I would have retired already. It's stiffer and tougher to work with than bread dough because there's less water in it—but the machine mixes it in a few minutes.

BI: Then what happens?

BB: Then the dough takes a little rest—10 minutes or so. You would too if you'd been mixed up like that. Also, that doughmixer is a very comfortable place to rest. It's always 78 to 80 degrees in there. We have to pamper the dough that way to keep the yeast happy.

BI: That dough does look very happy—like a big, spongy pillow. We wouldn't mind nestling in there ourselves. . . .

BB: Get out of my doughmixer! Anyway, that's enough rest time. We've got plenty of work ahead of us. Next we must divide and conquer! So into the divider it goes! You can see what happens there—the dough goes into it in one great lump and comes out in little, three-inch balls.

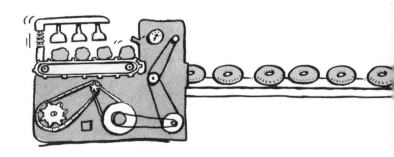

BI: They sure are cute. . . .

BB: No! They're not to play with! Put them down—they have to rest again.

BI: How do you get any work done with all this resting?

BB: It's not easy. But, as I said, we have to keep the dough happy. One thing I've learned in this business: Happy dough makes smiling bagels. That's my motto.

BI: The next machine looks scary! How does that keep the dough happy?

BB: That's the part it likes best! That's where it actually gets shaped into bagels. The balls of dough are massaged into strips. Then the strips get caught around a rod so that they turn into rings.

BI: That's one way to get into shape!

BB: You ain't seen nothing yet! Not only do they get a massage, but they also take a steam bath. Only we call the heated cubicle a proofer, not a steam bath. It's 110 degrees in there and the humidity is kept at 80 percent. That's the kind of climate yeast likes. In fact, it likes it so much that the rings of dough stay in there for 35 minutes and grow to double their original size. Also, that's where they learn to swim.

BI: You mean bagels know how to swim?

BB: They're real Olympic champions. Once they've risen, they dive right into a vat of boiling water. If they've risen enough, they float. First they float on one side for one minute; then they flip over and float on the other side for another minute.

BI: It sounds like you're running a gymnasium for bagels!

BB: Anything to keep them happy. Besides, bagels have to stay in shape. That little swim ensures that the bagel won't puff up and lose its attractive shape during baking. But you shouldn't think this is only recreation—the yeast is still working and making the bagel lighter as it swims.

BI: These bagels sound all wet to us!

BB: They are, but then they dry off on one side and flip into the oven. Because they land on their dry side, they don't stick to the hearth. Then comes the part I like best.

BI: What's that?

BB: All my dough turns to gold. The bagels go into the oven looking pale and puffy. Minutes later they come out looking tanned and glossy. They're so gorgeous you could eat them up!

BI: So we've noticed. . . .

BB: Go ahead—help yourself. Take as many as you want. . . .

BI: But what will we do with the ones we can't eat right away?

BB: I thought you'd never ask. We've discovered here that the best way to keep bagels on hand is to freeze them. So after all these plump, golden rings have cooled off a bit, we slice them and package them in plastic bags. Then they're frozen at 15 degrees below zero and kept frozen until you're ready to heat and enjoy them.

BI: You make it sound so easy. Have you encountered any problems with bagel baking?

BB: Have I had problems? Does a bagel have a hole? Of course there were problems.

BI: Tell us some of the obstacles you've encountered.

BB: Well, first there was the problem of finding a bagel shaper. It wasn't easy to find a manufacturer willing to make such equipment. It's not your common, everyday machinery, you know. And then there was the labor problem.

BI: You couldn't find anyone willing to make bagels?

BB: Oh, they were willing. If anything, they were too willing. Every time I hired a new baker, he wanted to help me improve the product. I had one guy—a Frenchman named Marcel—who thought he'd surprise me by making the dough lighter and leaving out the hole. He said I could make terrific *petits pains.* "But I don't want French bread," I hollered, "I want bagels!" So he figured I was doomed to failure and he left. Another guy, quite a good baker, tried to get me to convert to English muffins. And a lovely lady dumped sugar and eggs into the flour to improve my formula for doughnuts. I said, "Doughnuts? You're nuts! My customers want bagels!"

BI: So how did you solve this problem?

BB: I had 12 children. They solved the problem—they grew old enough to help me out.

BI: Do you see any new trends developing in the bagel baking business?

BB: Oh sure. There's always something new. Right now, pizza bagels are hot. And if things keep up the way they have been, who knows? We could be making taco bagels and bagels foo yong before long.

BI: Do you think the bagel can adapt to such changes?

BB: Of course. Bagels have been "a-round" for over 300 years. They're not suddenly going to become "square"!

BI: Of course not.

BB: And I'll tell you something else. . . .

BI: Yes?

BB: If you bake bagels long enough, before you know it you become a little crusty yourself!

BI: So we've noticed. Do you have any advice for would-be bagel bakers?

BB: Only one thing. If you play pinochle while the dough rises, watch out you don't lose your shirt!

If, armed with Mr. Bagelbaker's advice, you'd like to try your hand at bagel baking, here's a failsafe formula:

FRESH, HOT BAGELS

  1 package active dry yeast
1½ cups warm water (105°F to 115°F)
  3 tablespoons sugar
  1 tablespoon salt
  4 to 4½ cups all-purpose flour
  1 gallon water

1. Stir yeast into 1½ cups warm water in large bowl; let stand until bubbly, about 5 minutes. Stir in sugar, salt and enough flour to make soft dough. Knead dough on lightly floured board until smooth and elastic, adding remaining flour as necessary.

2. Let dough stand covered in warm place 15 minutes. Punch down dough; roll on lightly floured board to rectangle 13 x 4 inches (about 1-inch thick). Cut dough into 18 strips with floured knife. Roll each strip gently to form rope ½-inch thick; moisten ends and press together to form bagels. Place bagels on floured cookie sheets. Let stand covered 20 minutes.

3. Heat 1 gallon water to boiling in large saucepan; reduce heat to medium. Place 3 or 4 bagels in saucepan; simmer uncovered 7 minutes (no longer). Drain on towel. Repeat with remaining bagels.

4. Heat oven to 375°F. Bake bagels on ungreased cookie sheets until golden, 30 to 35 minutes. Cool on wire rack.

18 bagels

BAGEL NOTE: To top the bagels with poppy or sesame seeds, remove them from the oven after 10 minutes of baking. Brush them with 1 egg white beaten with 1 tablespoon water; sprinkle with seeds. Continue baking until golden.

THE BAGEL ADVISOR:
Frequently Asked Questions Concerning the Art and Etiquette of Eating Bagels

Q. What's the best way to toast a bagel?

A. There is no best way. It's strictly a matter of preference. Some people rely on a succession of noises to wake up in the morning. For them, the day doesn't truly begin until a radio announcer is barking out the news, the coffee pot is perking, the electric juicer is whining, the cereal is crackling and the toaster is popping. So naturally they prefer to drop their bagel into the toaster slots. Other people feel cruelly violated if they encounter so much as a loudly crumpled butter wrapper before they've had their second cup of coffee; so they quietly lay their bagel halves under the broiler. And, we're happy to report, there are still a few rugged individualists left who go out and gather kindling before breakfast so that they can toast their bagels before an open fire.

Q. Do you have to toast bagels?

A. No. Sometimes they're better untoasted. In fact, it's downright difficult to eat something squishy and highly mobile—like pastrami and cole slaw with Russian dressing—on a crisply toasted bagel. Bring out the bagel's most alluring fragrance, if you wish, by gently heating it in a low oven before you pile on the juicy filling. But save the toaster for clinging spreads and dips.

Q. What should I do when I want to pack a pastrami and cole slaw sandwich for my husband to take to work and the frozen bagel is like a rock?

A. There are several ways to deal with this dilemma. First, if you think about it the night before, you can leave the bagel to defrost in the refrigerator. Secondly, you can partially thaw the bagel in a low oven before you make the sandwich. Thirdly, you can make the sandwich on the frozen bagel; it will thaw out by lunchtime. You don't have to worry about the bagel getting soggy; it takes more than a scoop of cole slaw to penetrate a bagel. Whatever you do, however, don't toast a bagel if you don't plan to eat it right away—it tends to get a little . . . umm, stiff, if allowed to stand.

Q. Can I heat a bagel in the microwave oven?

A. It's not recommended. Bagels seem to toughen under the onslaught of microwaves.

Q. What can I do to revive a stale bagel?

A. Try moistening it slightly and baking it for ten minutes in a 350°F. oven. If that doesn't work, you might turn to "Artsy-Craftsy Bagels" on page 118. But if you'd rather not put good food to frivolous purposes, you can cut the bagel into chunks (if that's still possible—if not, you might as well settle for art!) and process the chunks into crumbs in a blender or food processor.

Q. What would I want with a bunch of bagel crumbs?

A. Don't let skepticism blind you to the infinite possibilities! You can sauté the crumbs in butter with herbs, mix them with grated Parmesan cheese and sprinkle them over cooked green vegetables. Or you can spice them with cinnamon and nutmeg to create a great topping for hot cereal or ice cream. Or you can combine them with melted butter and seasonings (three cups of crumbs to ¼ cup butter); then press the mixture into a pie or quiche pan and bake it for 10 minutes at 400°F. to make a sweet or savory pie crust. And when it's cold outside, you might share your bagel crumbs with the birds—but watch out that they don't start lobbying for cream cheese!

Q. I've heard that you can turn a stale bagel into bagel chips. Is this true?

A. It's true to a certain extent—that is, until the bagel petrifies. At that point a bagel cannot be salvaged. But until then, you can slice the bagel very thin, arrange it on a baking sheet, sprinkle it with seasoned salt and broil it until it's toasted. If you have a food processor, cut the bagel to fit the feed tube and use the regular slicing disc (not the thin one) to slice it.

Q. We've heard that bagels have magical properties? Have they been known to cure any diseases?

A. Yes. Loneliness. If you take out a bag of bagels in any public or semi-public place, you'll soon see what we mean.

Q. What is a "water bagel"?

A. It's just another name for a bagel. Although the term might conjure up an image of a sad, soggy ring, it refers only to the fact that all real bagels are boiled in water before they're baked.

Q. What's the difference between a "real" bagel and a fake bagel?

A. A real bagel is made of high-gluten flour and is shaped into a ring; it is boiled and hearth-baked to make it glossy, crusty and chewy. The telltale signs of a fake are: squared edges, no hole in the middle, a pallid crust and feathery lightness. A true bagel should offer some resistance when you bite into it; if it panders to a timid nibble, it's a fake.

Q. What does "hearth-baked" mean? Why is that supposed to make bread taste better?

A. "Hearth-baked" means that the dough is placed directly in the oven rather than in a pan. The absence of a pan makes the product crustier.

Q. Why do some people claim that the only real bagel is a plain bagel?

A. We have heard that claim bruited about and wish to state once and for all that there is no truth to it. Some otherwise intelligently self-indulgent people pride themselves on putting up a stoical show of willpower when it comes to things like poppy seeds, garlic and raisins. If they wish to confine their pleasure to plain bagels, they may do so. But we will not concede a single raisin!

Q. But aren't egg bagels different from real bagels?

A. It depends on how they're made. If they are simply unboiled, fluffy rolls that happen to be shaped into rings, they aren't real bagels. But if eggs are added to regular bagel dough for flavoring and the dough is both boiled and baked, then the product remains completely legitimate.

Q. Is there such a thing as an illegitimate bagel?

A. Yes.

Q. What makes a bagel illegitimate?

A. Hanky-panky.

Q. Does that mean that I can't take a bagel to a drive-in movie?

A. Not at all. In fact, the greatest date in bagel history was the time our friend Jeffrey took a bag of wheat 'n honeys to a double feature—or at least that's what Jeffrey claims.

Q. Why are bagels always the butt of dumb jokes?

A. We're not sure. But we'll tell you a good one we heard recently:

> A wealthy man asked his wife what she wanted for their anniversary. "An English butler," she replied. "And please ask him to arrange an intimate little celebration for just us and the Smiths."
>
> The butler was duly hired and instructed and the party arrangements were made. But when the wife came to check the dining table, she found that it was set for six. "But James," she said to the butler, "I told you it would be just us and the Smiths."
>
> "I know," the butler replied, in his veddy British tones. "But while you were out shopping this afternoon, Mrs. Smith called to say she'd be bringing the Bagels."

Q. Is there such a thing as a good bagel joke?

A. No comment.

Q. What is a bag of wheat 'n honeys, anyhow? And where can I get one?

A. Wheat 'n honey bagels are made with a high-fiber blend of whole wheat flour, wheat germ and whole grains. They're sweetened with honey and are somewhat denser than other bagels. You can pick up a bagful at your supermarket freezer case. But after that you're on your own. . . .

Q. Why do some people insist that bagels always be eaten with lox?

A. Mostly because they're especially fond of the combination. However, some people still cling to the peculiar notion that bagels were invented exclusively for lox, and vice versa. As far as we can tell, however, the marriage was not made in heaven. Indeed, one reliable source claims that bagels and lox only started going steady on Sunday brunch tables in America, where their mutual appearance came to signify New World prosperity. In Europe, bagels were most often consumed with butter.

Q. Can bagels be served instead of dinner rolls?

A. Absolutely. In fact, if we were to tout bagels as a symbol of prosperity, we'd pair them off with fillet mignon—which costs less than lox anyway.

Q. Why do people wear bagels around their necks? Is this some kind of weirdo sign?

A. People wear bagel necklaces to ward off frowns and other symptoms of pessimism. It may seem weird, but it works.

Q. What do you think of the practice of mating two kinds of bagels in one sandwich?

A. We think this is an excellent solution to the problem of which flavor bagel to choose. If you layer roast beef or cheese, for example, on half a garlic bagel and top it with half a pumpernickel bagel, you can savor the best of two worlds.

Q. Can a marriage last if one partner insists on eating bagels in bed?

A. It's possible, and certainly many such cases have been recorded. But it's much easier if both bed partners eat bagels together.

Q. Is it safe to give an infant a bagel to teethe on?

A. Not only is it safe, but some doctors recommend it. Let the bagel get a little stale first so that it will be less likely to crumble. And remember that the baby might have an easier time grasping a bagelette than a full-size bagel.

Q. Is it true that bagelettes were invented for people who lack the stamina for regular bagels?

A. No. Bagelettes were developed for all the indecisive people in the world, as well as all the dieters and the would-be Perle Mestas. You see, people who can't make up their minds about what to put on a regular bagel can double their choices with the half-size bagelettes. Dieters get only half the calories. And every host and hostess has the perfect base for canapés.

Q. My mother-in-law criticizes everything I do. She plans to visit us soon. I think bagels are my only hope. Can you suggest something I could do with them to please her?

A. Well, you could run off with them . . . but that's the cowardly way out. Short of that, we can only advise you to adopt the strategy we use with all ornery guests. Plan a brunch buffet laden with cheeses, sliced meat, smoked fish, potato salad, fruit salad and all manner of other mouth-watering morsels. Put out every kind of bagel as well as two or three kinds of bagel desserts. Fill every corner of the table with irresistible distractions. That way, we figure, the worst that can happen is that your mother-in-law will criticize your generosity. But it's more likely she'll feel so flattered by it all that she'll simply wave the white flag between bites.

Q. What beverage should I serve with bagels?

A. Choose beverages according to what you've put on or mixed with the bagels. If you've prepared an entree that has a distinctive foreign flavor, match it with the appropriate drink. For example, serve tea with Oriental food and white wine with Swiss fondues. Bring on the Chianti or Soave for Italian fare and beer for spicy curry blends. Other than that, it's up to you. Châteauneuf-du-Pape with chopped liver? Perhaps. But frankly we'd prefer a glass of seltzer.

Q. I am ten years old. I think frozen bagels make the best hockey pucks. My mother disagrees. Who is right?

A. We'd rather not get in the middle of that one.

Q. Why are bagels always described as "cheerful"? How can a roll with a hole be cheerful?

A. With that physiognomy, how can it afford not to be? Actually, however, the bagel's emotional status has been determined by scientific testing. We asked a carefully selected group of thousands of bageleaters to describe the expression on a bagel's face. Only two out of the thousands remained undecided; one replied "depends on whether it had a good day." Several dozen participants described the bagel as seductive. Six labeled the bagel's expression "quizzical." One person said, "filled with little fears and dreads." Another person wrote down "Most likely to succeed." And another filled in "Best dancer." But almost every single one of the other survey group members answered "cheerful" or some spelling thereof. (One person replied "mouthful" but his answer was disqualified as irrelevant.)

Q. Why does every bageleater consider himself or herself an expert on the subject?

A. Because every bageleater is an expert! It doesn't take much—just excellent taste and very strong jaw muscles.

Great Awakenings

Nothing gets us out of bed faster in the morning than the thought of a toasted bagel. A plain, golden bagel oozing melted butter. Or a hot wheat 'n honey reducing its crown of cream cheese to warm liquid satin. Or a ring of glossy egg bagel dripping marmalade.

In fact, we've been known to scurry out from under the covers dreaming of bagelettes. Only to discover, en route to the freezer, that it's three o'clock in the morning. And that we'd better chew very quietly and not bang the toaster or drop the butter knife.

But we know some slug-a-beds who won't lift an eyelid for anything but a rye bagel, with scrambled eggs and salami. Or an onion bagel draped with a couple of sunny-side-ups. Or a lox omelet on two pumpernickel rounds.

We've heard of people who won't even set their alarm clocks if there are no raisin 'n honey bagels to wake up to. And one lady we know never retires without first wrapping up sesame bagels spread with cream cheese and jam to sweeten the following day. Which is a much more thoughtful approach than that of the guy we know who won't admit it's morning until his wife whispers ''bagels'' in his ear.

What we can't understand, though, is the Sunday bagel brunch crowd. We know why they look forward to Sundays—and we certainly share their passion for heaping platters of cold cuts, smoked fish, salads, cheeses, fruit and eggs. What we can't figure out is how they manage to sleep until noon when there are bagels in the house!

With all due respect for both those who ''rise and shine'' and those who tumble out of bed a little tarnished, we present bagel breakfasts for every mood and appetite. If you're up early enough to polish an apple, try the Honey-of-an-Apple Omelet. Or beam a sunny ''Good morning'' at the prospect of Creamy Ham 'N Egg Bagels. But if you'd rather not be reminded that the day has begun, treat yourself kindly to a quick Red-Eye Special or an easy Patty on the Run.

28

"Stanley, you've been walking in your sleep again!"

Bagels 'n Eggs

THE BIG SCRAMBLE

Top a bagel with scrambled eggs. Garnish with a dollop of sour cream, strawberry preserves and mint sprig.

DOUBLE FRIED

Spoon sauteed onions over toasted bagel. Top with fried eggs; sprinkle with minced parsley.

POACHER'S PARADISE

Layer bagel with slice of ham and fried eggplant. Top with poached egg; sprinkle lightly with nutmeg.

DEVILISH DELIGHT

Top a toasted bagel with deviled egg halves. Bake 20 minutes at 300° F. Spoon hot cheese sauce over; sprinkle with paprika.

SALAMI SALUTE

Spread bagel with mustard. Top with eggs scrambled with sauteed onion, green pepper and salami. Sprinkle with minced parsley.

HONEY-OF-AN-APPLE OMELET

1 bagel *(wheat 'n honey),* cut into 1-inch pieces
2 tablespoons butter or margarine, melted
2 tablespoons brown sugar
½ teaspoon ground cinnamon
2 large apples, peeled, cored, thinly sliced
2 tablespoons butter or margarine
2 tablespoons honey
1 teaspoon lemon juice
2 tablespoons butter or margarine
8 eggs
½ cup milk
½ teaspoon salt
4 to 6 bagels *(wheat 'n honey),* toasted, buttered

1. Process bagel pieces in blender or food processor to make coarse crumbs; transfer to small bowl. Mix melted butter, sugar and cinnamon into crumbs.

2. Saute apples in 2 tablespoons butter in large skillet just until tender, about 5 minutes; transfer to medium bowl. Sprinkle with honey and lemon juice.

3. Heat oven to broil. Melt 2 tablespoons butter in large oven-proof skillet until bubbly. Beat eggs, milk and salt; pour into skillet. Cook over medium heat until eggs are set on bottom. Carefully lift edge of omelet with spatula to let uncooked portions of egg flow underneath. Cook until omelet is set, but still moist on top.

4. Spoon apple slices over top of omelet; sprinkle with bagel crumbs. Broil 4 inches from heat source until crumbs are browned, about 3 minutes. Transfer omelet to serving platter. Cut into wedges; serve with buttered bagels.

4 to 6 servings

BAGEL NOTE: Wheat 'n honey bagel crumbs mixed with melted butter, brown sugar and cinnamon give the Honey-of-an-Apple Omelet an irresistible crunchy topping. You can make the same crumb mixture, lightly toast it in the oven and serve it at breakfast time over fruit or hot cereal. You might want to make a double or triple batch and keep it refrigerated in a plastic bag or tightly covered jar. It tastes great on ice cream, too!

Bagels on the Run

RED-EYE SPECIAL

Spread bagel with chili sauce. Top with a ham
and onion slice and a fried egg.

APPLE PAN DANDY

Saute apple slices in butter until tender; spoon over
toasted bagel *(wheat 'n honey)*. Sprinkle with
cinnamon; top with crisply fried bacon.

LOX BEATS THE CLOCKS

Mix whipped cream cheese and dill weed; spread
on toasted bagel. Top with slices of onion and lox.

ANCHOVIES A-PLENTY

Spread a toasted bagel with butter and mashed
anchovies. Top with sliced hard-cooked egg and
rolled anchovy.

PATTY ON THE RUN

Butter toasted bagel. Spread with spicy brown
mustard and favorite preserves. Fill with cooked
sausage patty.

FRENCH TOAST À L'ORANGE

4 bagels *(sesame seed)*
2 eggs
½ cup milk
1 can (6 ounces) frozen orange juice
    concentrate, thawed
2 tablespoons sugar
½ teaspoon vanilla
    Pinch salt
3 tablespoons butter or margarine
⅔ cup pancake syrup
1 orange, peeled, cut into sections

1. Slice each bagel half in half horizontally. Mix eggs, milk, half the orange concentrate, the sugar, vanilla and salt in large shallow dish. Soak bagel slices in mixture 15 minutes on each side.

2. Heat butter in large skillet over medium heat. Fry bagel slices until golden, 3 to 5 minutes on each side.

3. Heat remaining orange concentrate, the pancake syrup and orange sections in small saucepan just to boiling. Overlap bagel slices on plates; spoon syrup over.

4 servings

CREAMY HAM 'N EGG BAGELS

2 tablespoons chopped green pepper
3 tablespoons butter or margarine
3 tablespoons all-purpose flour
½ teaspoon salt
¼ teaspoon dry mustard
¼ teaspoon pepper

1½ cups milk
3 hard-cooked eggs, chopped
1 can (4 ounces) sliced mushrooms,
    drained
1 cup cubed smoked ham
4 bagels *(rye),* toasted

1. Saute green pepper in butter in medium saucepan until tender, about 5 minutes. Stir in flour, salt, mustard and pepper; cook over medium heat, stirring constantly, 3 minutes. Stir in milk gradually; cook, stirring constantly, until thickened, about 5 minutes.

2. Stir eggs, mushrooms and ham into sauce; cook until hot, about 3 minutes. Arrange bagels on plates; spoon sauce over.

4 servings

LOX 'N BAGEL PIE

3 bagels *(onion),* cut into 1-inch pieces
¼ cup butter or margarine, melted
¼ teaspoon salt
1 small onion, finely chopped
2 tablespoons butter or margarine
5 eggs
2 cups milk
¼ teaspoon salt
⅛ teaspoon pepper
1 tablespoon chopped parsley
4 ounces shredded Swiss cheese
4 ounces sliced lox, cut into ½-inch
    pieces

1. Heat oven to 400° F. Process bagel pieces in blender or food processor to make fine crumbs. Mix crumbs with melted butter and ¼ teaspoon salt in greased 10-inch quiche pan; press mixture evenly on bottom and side of pan.

2. Bake until edges of crust begin to brown, 8 to 10 minutes. Cool on wire rack.

3. Saute onion in 2 tablespoons butter in small skillet until tender, about 5 minutes. Cool.

4. Reduce oven temperature to 350° F. Mix eggs, milk, ¼ teaspoon salt, the pepper, parsley and cooled onion. Sprinkle half the cheese on bottom of crust; pour egg mixture over cheese. Sprinkle lox and remaining cheese over all.

5. Bake until egg mixture is set and top is puffed and golden, 30 to 35 minutes. Let stand 10 minutes before cutting.

6 to 8 servings

BAGEL NOTE: The dense, rich lusciousness of Lox 'N Bagel Pie results from the perfect mating of a bagel crumb crust and a delicious filling of cheese, eggs and lox. This convenient party brunch dish can be served at room temperature. And you'll find that bagel crumb crusts, which can be made with other flavors of bagels too, improve upon ordinary pastry in all kinds of savory pies and quiches.

The Hearty Bagel

THE "HOLE" WORKS

Spread a bagel with whipped cream cheese. Top with slice of ham, sauteed mushrooms, a poached egg and Swiss cheese slice. Broil until cheese melts.

THE STEAK 'N EGGER

Top toasted bagel *(garlic)* with broiled steak and fried egg. Garnish with French-fried onion rings.

OYSTERS ON THE HALF-BAGEL

Toast bagel; top with lettuce leaf and fried breaded oysters. Sprinkle with lemon juice and red pepper sauce.

HASH-HOUSE BAGEL

Spoon hot corned beef hash over bagel. Top with green pepper ring and poached egg. Sprinkle with chopped chives.

RYES-AND-SHINE BAGEL

Top a toasted bagel *(rye)* with sauteed chicken livers and a poached egg. Sprinkle with chopped chives.

The Bagel Gourmet

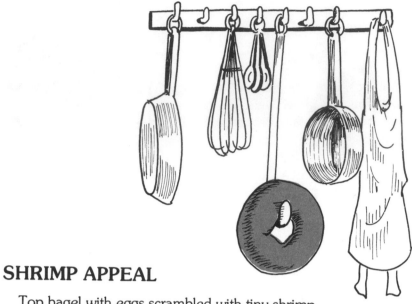

SHRIMP APPEAL

Top bagel with eggs scrambled with tiny shrimp. Garnish with sour cream and chopped chives.

CAVIAR CHIC

Spread bagel with cream cheese. Top with spoon of caviar; sprinkle with chopped green onion and hard-cooked egg.

FIT-FOR-A-KING CRAB

Mix cream cheese and crabmeat; spread on bagel *(poppy seed)*. Top with poached egg; sprinkle with capers.

HEAVENLY HOLLANDAISE

Top bagel with sauteed ham slice, cooked asparagus spears and poached egg. Spoon hollandaise sauce over; sprinkle with paprika.

AH, LUXURY!

Spread toasted bagel *(egg)* with butter. Top with sauteed sweetbreads; garnish with minced parsley and lemon wedge.

BAGELETTE BRUNCH BAKE

6 bagelettes *(onion),* toasted
12 eggs
⅔ cup milk
½ teaspoon salt
⅛ teaspoon pepper
½ cup finely chopped onion
¼ cup butter or margarine
½ cup finely chopped onion
⅓ cup butter or margarine
⅓ cup all-purpose flour
1¾ cups milk
4 ounces dried beef, cut into ¼-inch
    strips
1 can (4 ounces) sliced mushrooms,
    drained
⅛ teaspoon pepper
   Minced parsley

1. Place bagelettes, cut-sides up, on bottom of greased 7½ x 11¾-inch baking pan.

2. Beat eggs, ⅔ cup milk, the salt and ⅛ teaspoon pepper in large bowl. Saute ½ cup onion in ¼ cup butter in large skillet until tender, about 5 minutes. Add egg mixture to skillet; cook over low heat, stirring occasionally, until eggs are set but still soft. Spread eggs over bagelettes in baking dish.

3. Heat oven to 275° F. Saute ½ cup onion in ⅓ cup butter in medium saucepan until tender, about 5 minutes. Stir in flour; cook over medium heat, stirring constantly, 3 minutes. Stir in milk gradually; cook, stirring constantly, until thickened, about 5 minutes. Stir in beef, mushrooms and ⅛ teaspoon pepper. Spread mixture over eggs.

4. Bake covered 30 minutes. Uncover and sprinkle with parsley. Serve immediately.

6 servings

BAGEL NOTE: Four ounces of shredded Cheddar cheese can be substituted for the dried beef. You can assemble this hearty, one-dish brunch ahead of time, store it in the refrigerator and bake it ten minutes longer. The casserole cuts perfectly into six servings of two bagelette halves apiece. The recipe can be doubled or tripled and baked in two or three casseroles for large groups.

Better on a Bagel!

Everything tastes better on a bagel!

That was the unmistakable conclusion we drew from a recent poll of bagel sandwich eaters. Our first question, "What do you like to eat in a bagel sandwich?" drew so many and such varied responses that our statisticians went 'round in bagels trying to plot the results on a graph.

Answers ranged from tuna fish salad with lettuce, tomato, cheese and pickles to roast beef, pastrami, salami, turkey, tongue, chopped liver, olives, pimientos and onions (yes—all on one sandwich!). We found a definite correlation between income and such preferences as beluga on a bagel and bagels foie gras. But age seemed to have no bearing on the response of the seven bagel sandwich eaters who listed peanut butter, marshmallows and banana as their first choice.

The question "How do you eat a bagel sandwich?" split our survey group right down the middle. Half answered, "Open wide and take a big, big bite." The other half protested that civilized manners require a knife and fork. Strangely enough, there was no correlation between method and sandwich contents. The "open wide" group insisted that even coleslaw, tomatoes, ham and melted cheese taste better if both sandwich halves are lifted together in one big gamble of a bite. And the open-face sandwich devotees apparently ply their silverware even with cream cheese and jam.

Most surprising of all were the reasons listed under "Why do you like bagel sandwiches?" We had anticipated that many people would answer "Love that unique chewiness" or "The bagel never gets soggy." And we did get plenty of those responses. But what we never would have guessed was the number of people who treasure the feelings of strength, power, self-confidence and status that bagel sandwiches give them. Some examples:

Howard M., age 5, a prodigy in every way and table tennis champion of his block, recounted that bagels are the only kind of bread he can spread with peanut butter without tearing the slices.

George P., age 16, ninety-seven pounds and a gym-class dropout, reported that lifting six massive bagel sandwiches to his mouth daily was improving both his muscle power and his less-than-Herculean stature.

Marcia J., age 37, a secretary who had not received a salary increase in fifteen years, noted joyfully that her lunch of shrimp and artichokes on a bagel had so impressed her boss that he raised her wages immediately and asked her for a date.

We can't guarantee anything but eating pleasure with the sandwich recipes that follow. But our personal experience indeed confirms the view that everything tastes better on a bagel!

"You're supposed to lift 'em to your *mouth,* you dumbbell!

Bagel Bonanzas

THE BIG MOUTH SPECIAL

Mix mayonnaise and horseradish; spread on bagel. Layer with slices of pastrami, roast beef, salami, tomato and Brick cheese. Top with Russian dressing.

A FINE PICKLE

Combine equal parts of liverwurst and finely chopped dill pickle. Spoon onto lettuce on bagel *(pumpernickel)*; garnish with cherry tomato.

HAM 'N EGGER

Spread bagel with mayonnaise. Top with slice of baked ham and spinach leaves. Layer with egg salad; garnish with dill pickle.

BAGEL TARTARE

Make steak tartare; spread on bagel. Sprinkle with capers; top with raw egg yolk, if desired, and rolled anchovy.

GOING FISHIN'

Spread bagel *(egg)* with tartar sauce. Top with lettuce, baked or fried fish sticks and tomato slice. Garnish with lemon wedge.

EVERYTHING YOU EVER WANTED ON A BAGEL . . . BUT WERE AFRAID TO ASK

½ cup mayonnaise
1 teaspoon spicy brown mustard
1 tablespoon finely chopped onion
1 medium dill pickle, finely chopped
½ teaspoon celery seeds
　Dash pepper
2 cups finely chopped cabbage

4 slices Monterey Jack cheese
2 bagels
4 ounces sliced corned beef
8 slices liverwurst
4 dill pickles, sliced diagonally
4 radish roses

1. Mix mayonnaise, mustard, onion, chopped dill pickle, celery seeds and pepper; mix into cabbage in small bowl. Refrigerate covered several hours for flavors to blend.

2. Place cheese slices on bagels; spoon half the cabbage slaw on the cheese. Arrange beef on slaw; top with remaining slaw and the liverwurst.

3. Spear pickle slices and radishes on 4 toothpicks; place in top of each sandwich.

4 servings

REUBEN'S JUICY RELATIVE

1 pound bulk pork sausage
1 can (16 ounces) sauerkraut, drained
2 teaspoons caraway seeds
2 tablespoons brown sugar

2 tablespoons spicy brown mustard
2 bagels *(rye),* toasted
¼ cup thousand island dressing
4 slices Swiss cheese

1. Form sausage into 4 patties. Fry patties in skillet over medium heat until cooked and brown, about 5 minutes on each side. Drain on paper toweling.

2. Heat oven to 375° F. Mix sauerkraut, caraway seeds, brown sugar and mustard in small saucepan; heat until hot.

3. Spread bagels with dressing. Spoon half the sauerkraut on bagels; top with sausage patties, remaining sauerkraut and cheese. Wrap each bagel in aluminum foil.

4. Bake 20 minutes. Unwrap; serve hot.

4 servings

Connoisseur's Choice

SHRIMPLY DEVINE

Spread bagel with whipped cream cheese. Top with several shrimp and a dollop of cocktail sauce. Garnish with lemon wedge.

THE BEEF BARON

Toast bagel lightly; spread with spicy brown mustard. Add slices of rare roast beef; sprinkle with crumbled blue cheese.

FRUIT 'N CHEESY

Top a bagel (onion) with slice of fresh or canned pineapple and slice of Gruyēre cheese. Broil until cheese is bubbly; sprinkle with chives.

CHUT-NUT TURKEY

Mix chopped chutney and peanuts; spread on bagel. Top with thinly sliced breast of turkey; garnish with watercress.

ARTY CHOKE

Spread bagel (sesame seed) with cream cheese. Top with thinly sliced baked ham, tomato slice and marinated artichoke.

TUNA'S TOTAL TRIUMPH

1 can (6½ ounces) tuna in water, drained
4 small sweet pickles, finely chopped
2 green onions and tops, finely chopped
1 hard-cooked egg, finely chopped
½ cup coarsely chopped walnuts
½ cup mayonnaise
1 teaspoon prepared mustard

2 teaspoons lemon juice
¼ teaspoon salt
⅛ teaspoon pepper
8 slices tomato
2 bagels, toasted
½ cup shredded Cheddar cheese
    Paprika

1. Heat oven to 350° F. Mix tuna, sweet pickles, green onions, egg, walnuts, mayonnaise, mustard, lemon juice, salt and pepper in small bowl.

2. Place 1 tomato slice on each bagel half; spoon tuna mixture over tomatoes. Top with remaining tomato slices; sprinkle with cheese. Wrap each bagel in aluminum foil.

3. Bake 30 minutes. Unwrap bagels; place under broiler until cheese is bubbly, if desired. Sprinkle lightly with paprika. Serve hot.

4 servings

CHAMPION CHICKEN WALDORF

1½ cups cubed, cooked chicken
1 green onion and top, thinly sliced
1 apple, cored, cut into ½-inch pieces
1 rib celery, finely chopped
¼ cup golden raisins
¼ cup sliced almonds
½ cup mayonnaise
⅓ cup sour cream
1 tablespoon lemon juice
¼ teaspoon salt
⅛ teaspoon pepper
½ cup shredded lettuce
2 bagels *(sesame seed),* toasted,
    buttered
1 small carrot, shredded

1. Mix chicken, green onion, apple, celery, raisins, and almonds in medium bowl. Mix mayonnaise, sour cream, lemon juice, salt and pepper; stir into chicken mixture.

2. Arrange lettuce on bagels; spoon chicken mixture on lettuce. Garnish with shredded carrot.

4 servings

THERE'S NOTHING LIKE CHOPPED LIVER. . .

1½ pounds chicken livers, cleaned
½ cup vegetable oil
¼ cup chicken fat
2 medium onions, finely chopped
4 hard-cooked eggs, quartered
2 teaspoons salt
4 bagels *(onion)*
Radish slices

1. Cover chicken livers with water in medium saucepan; heat to boiling. Simmer uncovered over low heat 1½ hours. Drain.

2. Heat vegetable oil and chicken fat in large skillet; saute onions in skillet until tender, about 5 minutes. Remove skillet from heat; add chicken livers, eggs and salt. Mash livers and eggs with fork until mixture is well combined but still coarse in texture. Refrigerate covered until chilled.

3. Place generous spoon of chicken livers on bagels. Garnish with radish slices.

8 servings

. . . EXCEPT GREAT GEFILTE FISH!

3 tablespoons finely chopped onion
1 can (8 ounces) sliced beets, drained, rinsed, finely chopped
2 tablespoons red wine vinegar
½ teaspoon sugar
Dash pepper
4 ounces whipped cream cheese
1½ tablespoons prepared horseradish
2 bagels
4 pieces gefilte fish, each sliced crosswise into 8 slices
1 green onion and top, sliced
4 carrot curls

1. Mix chopped onion, beets, vinegar, sugar and pepper in small bowl; refrigerate covered several hours for flavors to blend.

2. Mix cream cheese and horseradish; spread on bagels. Spoon beet mixture on cream cheese. Arrange gefilte fish slices in attractive design on beets. Garnish with green onion slices and carrot curls.

4 servings

All The World Loves A Bagel

THAT'S A SPICY BAGEL!

Saute sliced fresh mushrooms in butter; spoon over bagel. Place large meatball in center; top with hot spaghetti sauce. Sprinkle with oregano and Parmesan cheese.

SCANDINAVIAN SKOAL

Top a bagel with generous layer of herring in sour cream. Sprinkle with finely chopped green onion; garnish with carrot curl.

TERIYAKI BAGEL

Spread bagel with butter. Top with thinly sliced roast beef. Sprinkle with teriyaki sauce, chopped green onion and sesame seeds.

BAGEL LUAU

Make chicken salad seasoned with a generous pinch of curry powder; spoon onto bagel (wheat 'n honey). Garnish with pineapple chunks and chopped cashews.

SOUTH-OF-THE-BAGEL

Mash ripe avocado; spread on bagel. Layer with tomato slice, chopped lettuce and onion and shredded Cheddar cheese. Garnish with dollop of sour cream.

Not For Kids Only

HOT-DIGGITY DOGS

Spread bagel *(onion)* with mustard. Top with
sliced grilled frankfurter and generous spoon of
hot baked beans.

SLOPPY MOE

Mix canned sloppy joe with shredded Cheddar
cheese; heat until cheese is melted. Spoon over
bagel *(egg);* top with sweet pickle slices.

BOLOGNA SMILES

Mix mayonnaise and mustard; spread on bagel.
Top with lettuce and bologna. Cut slice of cheese
into shapes and make "faces" on bologna.

BANANA SPLIT

Spread bagel *(raisin 'n honey)* with whipped cream
cheese. Top with banana slices, chopped nuts and
a spoon of strawberry preserves.

CHOCO-PEANUT MELT

Mix crunchy peanut butter and honey; spread on
bagel *(wheat 'n honey).* Sprinkle with chocolate
chips; broil until chocolate melts.

BETTER-THAN-BEEF BURGERS

1 pound ground chuck
¼ cup finely chopped onion
1 tablespoon Worcestershire sauce
½ teaspoon salt
¼ teaspoon pepper

¼ teaspoon garlic powder
4 slices liverwurst
4 ounces fresh mushrooms, sliced
2 tablespoons butter or margarine
2 bagels, toasted

1. Mix chuck, onion, Worcestershire, salt, pepper and garlic powder in medium bowl. Shape meat mixture into 8 patties that are 1-inch larger than liverwurst slices.

2. Place liverwurst slices on 4 of the meat patties; top with remaining meat patties. Press and seal edges of patties well.

3. Saute mushrooms in butter in medium skillet until mushrooms are tender, about 5 minutes. Grill burgers over charcoal, broil or pan fry as desired. Place burgers on bagels; top with mushrooms.

4 servings

SAUSAGE AND PEPPERS SUPREME

2 medium red onions, thinly sliced
2 tablespoons olive oil
2 medium green peppers, cut into ½-inch slices
2 medium red peppers, cut into ½-inch slices
¼ cup water

¼ teaspoon instant beef bouillon
1 teaspoon salt
¼ teaspoon pepper
4 medium tomatoes, cut into wedges
2 pounds hot or sweet Italian sausage, cut into 8 pieces
4 bagels *(garlic)*

1. Saute onions in olive oil in large saucepan until well browned, about 25 minutes. Stir in green and red peppers; cook over medium heat, stirring occasionally, 10 minutes.

2. Stir water, bouillon, salt and pepper into saucepan; simmer covered, stirring occasionally, 45 minutes. Stir in tomatoes; simmer uncovered until mixture is thick, 20 to 30 minutes.

3. Grill, broil or pan fry sausage until done. Spoon half the pepper mixture on bagels; top with sausage and remaining pepper mixture. Serve hot.

8 servings

Dinner in the Round

We're thinking of opening up a cooking school. Not one of those glitzy, gourmet affairs devoted to soufflés, stockpots and such. Not a pleasure palace where students whip up dreams from air and egg whites, nor a fire station dedicated to the art of flambé. Instead, our classes could be labeled "Cooking in the Combat Zone."

There would be no fancy copper cookware in our classroom kitchen, no matching sets of pots and pans, no neatly arrayed whisks and spoons. Not only would the cookpots be dented, the stovetop slanted and the counterspace cramped, but we would conduct all lessons under simulated dinner-hour conditions. There would always be one slightly grimy, strong-lunged child around to whine "When are we going to eeeee-eat?" And another to peer over students' shoulders and sniff "Meatloaf again?" or to sound the alarm "You know I hate pot roast!" While one bystander would drag out a bag of potato chips to chomp a rhythmic chorus with the chopping knives. And another would swing the refrigerator door open and shut like a predinner pendulum.

In short, we would offer lessons not only in cooking but also in self-defense. Sessions would tackle such topics as: Crowd Control in the Inner Kitchen; Appeasing the Pot-Roast Picket Line; Handling the Invasion of the Cookie-Snatchers; Meeting the Challenge of Yesterday's Chicken Today; and The Race Against Time, or How to Serve Dinner Before They Serve Themselves Peanut Butter Sandwiches.

How, you might ask, can we presume to placate that most aggressive breed, Very Hungry People, on their own turf?

Our answer, of course, is bagels. The glossy rings come to the fore once again—both as a not-so-secret ingredient and as a failsafe weapon.

Here is our strategy: When the youngest starvelings start giving you that warning stare of dull-eyed deprivation, hand them the bagels and a butter knife and tell them they can speed things along by preparing the dinner rolls (and if they snitch one along the way, that's OK too). When the chicken stares back at you with discomforting familiarity, stuff it with an irresistible mix of bagels and savory herbs. If the anti-pot roast lobby has protested your previous efforts, sauce the source of their discontent with an unbeatable bagel blend. And when everyone craves a change-of-pace meal but meat prices counsel caution, try marvelous Bagel Brochettes or Barbecue on a Bagel.

No doubt our tactics invite skepticism, but nevertheless, if you love to dine well you won't be disappointed in the recipes for Dinner in the Round.

"Can I help, too?"

The Bagel Goes Big Time

POULET MORNAY

Spread bagel with whipped cream cheese. Top with cooked asparagus spears and baked chicken breast. Spoon cheese sauce over; garnish with parsley.

HIGH STEAKS

Spoon sauteed chopped onion, green pepper and tomato over toasted bagel *(rye)*. Arrange sliced broiled flank steak on top; sprinkle with salt, pepper and crumbled blue cheese. Broil until cheese melts, about 1 minute.

PORKY PRODIGY

Spread bagel with butter; top with apple ring, sauteed mushrooms and roast pork slices. Spoon cream gravy over; garnish with sauteed mushroom caps.

LAMB KARMA

Sprinkle buttered bagel *(egg)* with curry powder. Top with thinly sliced roast lamb. Spoon plain yogurt mixed with chopped cucumber and mint over; garnish with cucumber and tomato slices sprinkled with curry.

SALMON SHOW-STOPPER

Mix whipped cream cheese with dill weed; spread on bagel. Top with cucumber slices and broiled salmon steak. Spoon hollandaise sauce over; sprinkle with paprika.

BARBECUE ON A BAGEL

1 small onion, finely chopped
2 tablespoons butter or margarine
1 cup tomato sauce
¼ cup catsup
¼ cup honey
1 tablespoon dark molasses
1 tablespoon soy sauce
1 teaspoon Worcestershire sauce

½ teaspoon dry mustard
⅛ teaspoon ground ginger
⅛ teaspoon ground cloves
⅛ teaspoon garlic powder
Dash red pepper sauce
½ pound sliced rare roast beef
2 bagels *(garlic),* toasted

1. Saute onion in butter in medium saucepan until well browned, about 15 minutes. Stir in remaining ingredients except roast beef and bagels. Simmer uncovered until sauce has thickened to desired consistency, about 30 minutes.

2. Cut beef into ½-inch strips; stir into sauce. Cook, stirring occasionally, until beef is hot, 5 to 8 minutes. Serve hot on bagels.

2 servings

BAGEL BROCHETTES

½ cup red wine vinegar
½ cup vegetable oil
¼ teaspoon dried basil leaves
¼ teaspoon dried oregano leaves
½ teaspoon Dijon-style mustard
1 teaspoon minced parsley
¼ teaspoon garlic powder
½ teaspoon salt
⅛ teaspoon pepper

¾ pound boneless beef round or sirloin steak, cut into 1-inch cubes
4 bagelettes, cut into quarters
1 large green pepper, cut into 1-inch pieces
16 fresh mushrooms
8 cherry tomatoes
4 cups hot cooked rice

1. Mix vinegar, oil, basil, oregano, mustard, parsley, garlic, salt and pepper; pour over meat cubes in shallow dish. Refrigerate covered several hours, stirring occasionally. Drain; reserve marinade.

2. Alternate meat cubes, bagelettes, green pepper, mushrooms and tomatoes on 8 skewers. Grill over charcoal or broil to desired doneness, brushing frequently with reserved marinade. Serve on rice.

4 to 6 servings

STUFFING ITALIANO

3 cups cubed, peeled eggplant
Salt
3 bagels *(garlic),* cut into ½-inch pieces
⅔ cup chopped onion
1 small tomato, seeded, chopped
⅓ cup melted butter or margarine
¼ cup chicken broth
2 teaspoons lemon juice
2 tablespoons grated Parmesan cheese
½ teaspoon dried basil leaves
½ teaspoon dried oregano leaves
½ teaspoon salt

1. Sprinkle eggplant generously with salt; let stand 20 minutes. Rinse thoroughly and drain. Squeeze out excess moisture.

2. Mix all ingredients in large bowl. Use as stuffing for poultry or veal breast or bake at 350° F. in covered casserole 1 hour.

About 6 cups

COUNTRY COUSIN STUFFING

1 pound bulk pork sausage
1 cup chopped celery
½ cup chopped onion
½ cup sliced fresh mushrooms
3 bagels, cut into ½-inch pieces
⅓ cup chicken broth
¼ cup melted butter or margarine
½ teaspoon dried sage leaves
½ teaspoon poultry seasoning
½ teaspoon salt

1. Cook sausage in medium skillet over low heat until brown, about 10 minutes. Add celery and onion; cook over medium heat until onion is tender, about 5 minutes.

2. Combine all ingredients in large bowl. Use as stuffing for poultry or pork chops or bake at 350° F. in covered casserole 1 hour.

About 6 cups

THE BIRD THAT ATE THE BAGELS

"Boy am I stuffed!"

2 bagels *(pumpernickel),* cut into
    ½-inch pieces
¼ cup butter or margarine
2 ribs celery, finely chopped
2 small carrots, finely chopped
2 small onions, finely chopped
⅓ cup butter or margarine
½ pound fresh mushrooms, sliced
⅔ cup chopped toasted walnuts

½ teaspoon dried sage leaves
½ teaspoon dried thyme leaves
½ teaspoon caraway seeds
½ teaspoon salt
¼ teaspoon pepper
1 roasting chicken, about 3 pounds
¼ teaspoon salt
¼ teaspoon pepper

1. Saute bagel pieces in ¼ cup butter in large skillet until golden, about 3 minutes; transfer to large bowl. Saute celery, carrots and onions in ⅓ cup butter until onions are tender, about 8 minutes. Add mushrooms to skillet; cook 2 minutes. Add mixture to bagels.

2. Heat oven to 325° F. Stir walnuts, sage, thyme, caraway seeds, ½ teaspoon salt and ¼ teaspoon pepper into vegetable mixture; blend thoroughly. Sprinkle chicken cavity with ¼ teaspoon salt and ¼ teaspoon pepper. Fill cavity with stuffing; truss chicken. Place chicken on rack in roasting pan.

3. Roast until chicken leg moves easily and juices are clear when thigh is pierced with fork, 1¼ to 1½ hours. Baste occasionally with pan juices. Transfer to serving platter.

4 servings

BAGEL NOTE: Any extra stuffing can be spooned into a casserole and baked covered 1 hour.

Better than a Dinner Roll . . .
Bagel Hot Breads

TOMATO PAISANO

Mix tomato sauce with dried oregano and basil leaves; spread on bagel *(garlic).* Sprinkle with Parmesan cheese. Broil until bubbly, about 1 minute. Serve with grilled hamburgers or Italian sausage.

HERBIE BAGEL

Stir dried tarragon leaves into mayonnaise; spread on bagel *(egg).* Broil until brown, about 1 minute. Serve with roast meat, poultry or fish.

BAGEL CAPERS

Spread bagel *(poppy seed)* with butter; press capers into butter. Broil until toasted, about 1 minute. Serve with baked or broiled fish.

CARAWAY RINGS

Mix whipped cream cheese with caraway seeds. Spread on bagel. Broil until cheese melts, about 1 minute. Serve with stuffed cabbage or sauerbraten.

BEEFEATER BAGELS

Cream butter with minced green onions and tops and a dash of Worcestershire sauce; spread on bagel. Broil until toasted, about 1 minute. Serve with steak or roast beef.

BEST OF ALL POSSIBLE BRISKETS

2 large onions, chopped
½ cup vegetable oil
2 tablespoons instant beef bouillon
1 can (16 ounces) sauerkraut, undrained
¼ cup dark raisins
2 large apples, pared, cored, coarsely
  chopped
½ pound carrots, cut into ¼-inch slices
1 teaspoon brown sugar
2½ teaspoons salt
2 teaspoons pepper
1 can (15 ounces) tomato sauce
1 can (12 ounces) beer
2 tablespoons brown sugar
1 tablespoon instant beef bouillon
1 beef brisket (about 4 pounds)
½ teaspoon salt
3 bay leaves
2 bagels *(rye),* cut into 1-inch pieces

"It's a Dutch oven."

1. Saute onions in oil in Dutch oven until tender, about 5 minutes. Sprinkle onions with 2 tablespoons bouillon; cook over medium heat until onions are very brown. Stir in sauerkraut and liquid and raisins; cook, stirring occasionally, 10 minutes.

2. Stir in apples; cook until apples are soft, about 10 minutes. Add carrots; cook, stirring occasionally, 10 minutes. Stir in 1 teaspoon sugar, 2½ teaspoons salt and the pepper; cook, stirring constantly, 5 minutes.

3. Combine tomato sauce, beer, 2 tablespoons sugar and 1 tablespoon bouillon; reserve.

4. Heat oven to 325° F. Place brisket in Dutch oven; sprinkle with ½ teaspoon salt. Spoon onion mixture over beef; pour in tomato mixture. Add bay leaves. Cover Dutch oven with aluminum foil and lid.

5. Bake 2 hours. Process bagel pieces in blender or food processor to make fine crumbs. Stir into Dutch oven. Bake covered until beef is tender, 2 to 2½ hours.

6. Transfer beef to platter. Slice across grain; serve with gravy.

8 servings

BAGEL NOTE: The bagel crumbs thicken the savory brisket gravy to perfect consistency. They'll do the same for pot roasts and stews, too.

SKEWERED BAGEL LOAF

½ cup butter or margarine
1 clove garlic, minced
2 teaspoons minced parsley
¼ teaspoon dried basil leaves
¼ teaspoon dried oregano leaves
¼ teaspoon dried thyme leaves
¼ teaspoon dried marjoram leaves
¼ teaspoon onion powder
¼ teaspoon pepper
6 bagels

1. Heat oven to 350° F. Melt butter in small saucepan. Stir remaining ingredients, except bagels, into butter. Cook over low heat 2 minutes.

2. Spoon butter over bagels. Arrange bagels on skewer, with cut sides facing in same direction; wrap in aluminum foil. Place on baking sheet.

3. Bake 30 minutes. Remove foil; serve hot.

6 servings

BAGEL NOTE: The convenience of the pre-sliced bagels makes this herb-fragrant loaf especially attractive for barbecues and buffet tables.

. . . And More Bagel Hot Breads!

TANGY TOASTS
Spread bagel with butter and mustard; sprinkle with dill weed. Broil until toasted, about 1 minute. Serve with corned beef or brisket.

ORIENT EXPRESS
Brush bagel generously with Teriyaki sauce; spread with butter. Broil until toasted, about 1 minute. Serve with grilled meats or stir-fried dishes.

FISHERMAN'S FEAST

2 medium onions, finely chopped
2 cloves garlic, minced
2 tablespoons butter or margarine
2 tablespoons olive oil
1 rib celery, chopped
1 medium red potato, peeled, julienned
1 cup peeled, julienned eggplant
1 can (28 ounces) tomatoes, undrained
4 cups water
1 cup dry white wine
¼ teaspoon red pepper flakes
¼ teaspoon dried oregano leaves
¼ teaspoon dried basil leaves
¼ teaspoon dried thyme leaves
¼ teaspoon fennel seeds
1 bay leaf
1 pound cod fillets, cut into 2-inch
   pieces
2 tablespoons minced parsley
¾ teaspoon salt
1 tablespoon lemon juice
4 bagels (garlic)
  Olive oil
½ cup grated Parmesan cheese

1. Saute onions and garlic in butter and 2 tablespoons oil in Dutch oven 3 minutes. Stir in celery, potato and eggplant; saute until celery is tender, about 5 minutes. Add tomatoes and liquid, water, wine, pepper flakes, oregano, basil, thyme, fennel and bay leaf. Heat to boiling. Simmer covered on low heat 30 minutes.

2. Stir in cod, parsley, salt and lemon juice. Simmer uncovered until fish is tender, 5 to 9 minutes.

3. Heat oven to broil. While fish is cooking, brush bagels with olive oil; sprinkle with Parmesan cheese. Broil until golden, about 1 minute. Place bagels in bottoms of individual shallow bowls. Ladle soup into bowls.

8 servings
(about 1½ cups each)

BAGEL NOTE: The oil and cheese seasoned bagels add savor and substance to the fish broth. You can use them to enrich minestrone and other hearty soups as well.

57

CABBAGE WRAPS IT UP

2 cups chopped onions
2 tablespoons butter or margarine
2 bagels *(pumpernickel)* cut into 1-inch
    pieces
1 pound ground veal or pork
1 pound ground beef
2 tablespoons brown sugar
1 tablespoon lemon juice
2 tablespoons minced parsley
½ teaspoon caraway seeds
¼ teaspoon dried thyme leaves
½ teaspoon salt
⅛ teaspoon pepper
12 large cabbage leaves
1 can (8 ounces) tomato sauce
⅓ cup chicken broth
⅔ cup sour cream, optional

1. Saute onions in butter in large skillet until tender, about 5 minutes.

2. Process bagel pieces in blender or food processor to make coarse crumbs. Combine crumbs, onions, veal, beef, brown sugar, lemon juice, parsley, caraway seeds, thyme, salt and pepper in large bowl; mix thoroughly.

3. Cover cabbage leaves with hot water in large saucepan. Heat to boiling; cook until leaves are softened, about 3 minutes. Drain.

4. Heat oven to 375° F. Divide meat mixture on cabbage leaves; roll up, tucking in sides of leaves. Place seam-sides down in ungreased baking pan. Pour tomato sauce and broth over rolls. Cover tightly with aluminum foil.

5. Bake 1 hour. Arrange cabbage rolls on platter. Stir sour cream into sauce in pan; heat over low heat 2 to 3 minutes. Pour sauce over cabbage rolls.

6 servings

BAGEL NOTE: If sour cream is omitted, serve cabbage rolls and sauce over bagel halves. Bagel crumbs keep the meat filling of these cabbage rolls wonderfully moist. You can add bagel crumbs to meatloaf or meatballs for equally delicious results.

Naturally, It's a Bagel!

The trend to natural foods has taken many people we know by surprise. It seems, you see, that what's deemed "natural" by one school of thought seems rather peculiar to those accustomed to another.

Like our old friend Eddie, for instance, who thought it only natural that meals consist solely of meat and potatoes. So he couldn't understand why his wife began to insist on sullying his diet with salads—or "grass clippings," as he called them.

Or our neighbor Thelma, who fainted when her son told her he needed some "green stuff" and protested, when she pulled out her purse, that he meant not money but spinach!

Or Jack, who accused his wife of cheating on him when she substituted ground lima beans for beef in the meatloaf she had been serving him every Thursday for twenty-five years.

On the other hand, however, there's our friend Lorraine, who lured her boyfriend into proposing marriage by plying him daily with organically grown treats. When asked to explain his turnabout, the heretofore confirmed bachelor explained, "It's only natural, of course!"

We've been into natural foods for years. So the only thing that astonishes us is that they didn't appeal to the popular appetite sooner. By "natural," we mean nutritious and unadulterated by chemical additives and preservatives. Like fresh salads and vegetables, fruits, grains, beans, nuts and many dairy products. And, especially, bagels. For this chewy, hearthbaked bread has no preservatives or artificial flavorings among its ingredients; it retains its fresh, natural goodness solely through freezing.

While we haven't abandoned meat, fish or eggs in favor of vegetarian fare exclusively, we have turned increasingly to other sources of vitamins and protein. So you'll find meatless entrées as well as tempting and satisfying salads and sidedishes in our "holesome" garden of recipes.

"Holesome" Combinations

HEALTHNUT BAGEL
Mix softened cream cheese with shredded carrot, chopped nuts, raisins and honey; spread on bagel. Garnish with carrot curl.

SPROUTED BAGEL
Top buttered bagel with tomato slice and slice of Muenster cheese. Broil until bubbly. Sprinkle with alfalfa sprouts.

SUNSHINE BAGEL
Spread bagel (sesame seed) with cream cheese mixed with honey. Top with peeled orange slice; sprinkle with finely crushed gingersnaps.

TROPICAL BAGEL
Combine cottage cheese with crushed pineapple and minced mint leaves; spread on bagel (raisin 'n honey). Garnish with slice of kiwi.

MEDITERRANEAN BAGEL
Mix whipped cream cheese with chopped ripe olives and chopped walnuts. Spread on bagel; top with hard-cooked egg slices.

CHINESE STIR-FRIED VEGETABLES

3 tablespoons peanut or vegetable oil
1 carrot, cut diagonally into ¼-inch slices
1 rib celery, cut diagonally into
    ¼ inch slices
1 clove garlic, minced
½ teaspoon minced ginger root
1 cup shredded Chinese cabbage
1 cup sliced fresh mushrooms
1 cup fresh bean sprouts, rinsed, drained
4 ounces fresh snow peas, ends trimmed,
    strings removed

1 can (6½ ounces) water chestnuts,
    drained, sliced
2 green onions and tops, cut diagonally
    into 1-inch slices
1 tablespoon soy sauce
1 tablespoon water
2 tablespoons dry sherry
1 teaspoon cornstarch
4 bagels *(sesame),* toasted

1. Heat oil in wok or large skillet until hot. Add carrot, celery, garlic and ginger root; stir-fry 3 minutes. Add cabbage; stir-fry 2 minutes. Add mushrooms, bean sprouts, snow peas, water chestnuts and green onions; stir-fry 3 minutes.

2. Mix soy sauce, water, sherry and cornstarch; stir into vegetables. Stir-fry until vegetables are crisp-tender and sauce thickened, about 2 minutes. Serve over bagels.

4 servings

GOLDEN ZUCCHINI BOATS

2 bagels *(egg),* cut into 1-inch cubes
4 medium zucchini, cut lengthwise in half
1 package (3 ounces) cream cheese,
    room temperature
¼ cup grated Parmesan cheese
2 tablespoons melted butter or margarine

2 tablespoons minced parsley
½ teaspoon dried tarragon leaves
½ teaspoon salt
⅛ teaspoon pepper
1 cup shredded Cheddar cheese
    Paprika

1. Process bagel pieces in blender or food processor to make coarse crumbs. Scoop pulp from zucchini; chop coarsely. Mix bagel crumbs, chopped zucchini, cream cheese, Parmesan cheese, butter, parsley, tarragon, salt and pepper in medium bowl.

2. Heat oven to 350° F. Fill zucchini shells with mixture; place in greased baking pan. Bake uncovered 45 minutes. Sprinkle with Cheddar cheese; bake until cheese is melted, about 5 minutes. Sprinkle with paprika.

4 servings

SLICK-AS-A-CHICK PEA DIP

1 can (15 ounces) chick peas, drained,
    rinsed
2 cloves garlic, minced
⅓ cup peanuts
½ to ⅔ cup olive oil
¼ teaspoon salt
    Olive oil
    Minced mint leaves
4 bagels, cut into 1-inch pieces,
    toasted

1. Process chick peas, garlic and peanuts in blender or food processor until smooth, adding up to ⅔ cup oil for desired dipping consistency. Stir in salt. Refrigerate covered several hours for flavors to blend.

2. Spoon dip into bowl; drizzle top with olive oil. Sprinkle with mint. Serve at room temperature with bagels for dippers.

About 2¼ cups

DILLY-OF-A-YOGURT DIP

8 ounces plain yogurt
½ cup sour cream
1 small cucumber, peeled, seeded,
    chopped
1 teaspoon honey
1 tablespoon minced parsley
2 teaspoons dried dill weed
½ teaspoon salt
⅛ teaspoon pepper
4 bagels, cut into 1-inch pieces,
    toasted

1. Mix all ingredients except bagels in small bowl. Refrigerate covered several hours for flavors to blend.

2. Spoon dip into bowl. Serve chilled with bagels for dippers.

About 2 cups

SUBLIME-A-LIMA LOAF

1 medium onion, finely chopped
1 rib celery, finely chopped
¼ cup butter or margarine
1 bagel, cut into 1-inch pieces
2 cans (15 ounces each) lima beans, drained, rinsed
½ cup chopped walnuts
2 tablespoons minced parsley
1 egg

½ cup whipping cream
¼ teaspoon dried rosemary leaves
¼ teaspoon dried thyme leaves
¼ teaspoon dried sage leaves
½ teaspoon salt
⅛ teaspoon pepper
1 can (8 ounces) tomato sauce
1 cup sliced fresh mushrooms
1 cup shredded Swiss cheese

1. Saute onion and celery in butter in skillet until onion is tender, about 5 minutes. Cool.

2. Process bagel pieces in blender or food processor to make fine crumbs. Process lima beans in blender or food processor until smooth. Mix onion mixture, bagel crumbs, beans, walnuts, parsley, egg, cream, rosemary, thyme, sage, salt and pepper in medium bowl.

3. Heat oven to 350° F. Form bean mixture into loaf in greased 6-cup loaf pan; cover with aluminum foil. Bake 30 minutes. Remove foil; bake 45 minutes. Let cool 10 minutes.

4. While bean loaf is baking, simmer tomato sauce and mushrooms in small saucepan 20 minutes, stirring frequently. Add cheese; stir until melted.

5. Unmold bean loaf on serving platter. Slice and serve with tomato sauce.

8 servings

BAGEL NOTE: The lima beans, walnuts and Swiss cheese make this flavorful loaf a protein-rich meat substitute.

MANY-SPLENDORED SPINACH SALAD

1 cup cottage cheese
¼ cup crumbled blue cheese
2 tablespoons lemon juice
¼ teaspoon salt
⅛ teaspoon pepper
1 cup vegetable oil
1 bagel, cut into 1-inch pieces

6 cups shredded spinach
2 hard-cooked eggs, cut into
   quarters
1 cup julienned cooked beets
1 medium cucumber, scored,
   thinly sliced
1½ cups alfalfa sprouts, rinsed, drained

1. Process cheeses, lemon juice, salt and pepper in blender or food processor until smooth. Add oil slowly, processing until smooth. Refrigerate covered until chilled.

2. Heat oven to broil. Process bagel in blender or food processor to make coarse crumbs. Spread crumbs on cookie sheet; broil until toasted, stirring frequently. Set aside.

3. Arrange spinach in shallow salad bowl; arrange remaining ingredients attractively over spinach. Sprinkle top of salad with reserved crumbs. Serve with dressing.

4 servings

BAGEL IN THE BERRY PATCH

Mix mashed ripe strawberries and whipped cream cheese; spread on bagel (wheat 'n honey). Top with sliced strawberries and chopped fresh mint.

BANANA-MANNA BAGEL

Mash banana with sour cream, honey and cinnamon; spread on bagel. Press blueberries into mixture. Place under broiler until hot, about 1 minute.

GLORIOUS GARDEN SALAD

½ pound cauliflower, cut into flowerets
½ pound green beans, ends trimmed
½ pound asparagus, stalks trimmed
½ pound carrots, cut into ¼-inch slices
1 cup olive oil
¼ cup red wine vinegar
2 tablespoons lemon juice

1 teaspoon Dijon-style mustard
½ cup finely chopped onion
½ teaspoon dried basil leaves
½ teaspoon salt
⅛ teaspoon pepper
4 bagels
Lettuce leaves

1. Cook cauliflower, green beans, asparagus and carrots in steamer until crisp-tender.

2. Mix oil, vinegar, lemon juice, mustard, onion, basil, salt and pepper; pour over vegetables in medium bowl. Refrigerate covered several hours or overnight for flavors to blend.

3. Heat oven to broil. Slice bagels very thinly by hand or in food processor. Spread slices on cookie sheet; broil until toasted on both sides.

4. Line salad bowl with lettuce leaves; spoon vegetable mixture into bowl. Serve with bagel slices.

4 to 6 servings

CURRY COMBO
Mix chopped chutney and curry powder; spread on bagel. Sprinkle generously with coconut; broil until browned, about 1 minute.

NUT CRUNCH
Spread bagel (raisin 'n honey) with butter; dip into finely chopped pecans, walnuts or cashews. Broil until toasted, about 1 minute.

EGGPLANT CAVIAR

1½ cups cubed, peeled eggplant
    Salt
¼ cup finely chopped onion
1 clove garlic, minced
¼ cup olive oil
1 small tomato, peeled, seeded, finely
    chopped
½ cup chopped, toasted almonds
2 tablespoons minced parsley
½ teaspoon lemon juice
¼ teaspoon salt
4 bagels *(garlic),* cut into 1-inch
    pieces, toasted

1. Sprinkle eggplant generously with salt; let stand 20 minutes. Rinse thoroughly and drain. Squeeze out excess moisture.

2. Saute onion and garlic in olive oil in medium skillet until onion is tender, about 3 minutes. Stir in eggplant; cook over medium heat until eggplant is soft, about 5 minutes. Mash mixture with fork.

3. Stir remaining ingredients except bagels into eggplant mixture. Refrigerate covered several hours for flavors to blend.

4. Spoon mixture into bowl. Serve at room temperature with bagels for dippers.

About 1¾ cups

BAGEL NOTE: Eggplant Caviar is an old Russian favorite that's sometimes called "poor man's caviar." For special "dippers," spread bagels with butter and sprinkle with paprika before cutting and toasting. Or add a piquant touch by sprinkling buttered bagels with chili powder and chopped parsley before toasting under broiler.

FALAFEL

1 small onion, finely chopped
1 clove garlic, minced
¼ cup olive oil
1 bagel, cut into 1-inch pieces
1 can (15 ounces) chick peas, drained, rinsed
¼ cup wheat germ
¼ cup minced parsley
1 teaspoon minced mint leaves
1 egg
¼ teaspoon ground cumin
⅛ teaspoon ground mace
¼ teaspoon salt
¼ cup unbleached flour
Vegetable oil
Lettuce leaves
1¼ cups plain yogurt
2 tablespoons minced mint leaves

1. Saute onion and garlic in ¼ cup oil in skillet until onion is tender, about 5 minutes. Cool.

2. Process bagel in blender or food processor to make fine crumbs. Process chick peas in blender or food processor until smooth. Mix all ingredients except vegetable oil, lettuce leaves, yogurt and 2 tablespoons mint in medium bowl. Shape mixture into 24 balls.

3. Heat 1-inch vegetable oil to 350° F. in skillet. Cook falafel in oil until brown on all sides, about 2 minutes. Drain on paper toweling.

4. Arrange lettuce on serving plate; top with falafel. Mix yogurt and 2 tablespoons mint; spoon over falafel.

4 servings

BAGEL NOTE: Falafel are a crisp and mouthwatering Middle Eastern treat; served with yogurt topping they are a nutritious meat substitute. Without the yogurt sauce and speared with toothpicks, they make a great cocktail accompaniment.

Say Cheese!
Say Bagels!

It's almost as hard to say "bagels" without giggling as it is to say "cheese" without flashing a grin. So we knew when we invited our friends to a bagels and cheese tasting party that the invitations might generate a chuckle or two. But the success of the event exceeded even our highest expectations.

Casual get-togethers, you see, had become somewhat of a problem in recent years. Our old friends have developed different tastes, separate interests and widely varying ideas of what constitutes a good time. Whereas beer, pretzels and gossip used to satisfy just about everyone, that formula has failed miserably ever since Joe and Madeleine visited Paris and became connoisseurs of French wine and bon mots. And Melvin and Claire took up jogging and high-protein diets. And Hal and Elaine got into transcendental meditation and gave up beer. And Leroy's therapist told Leroy it was okay to bring chocolate milk and cookies to parties if that's what made him happy. Whereupon Madeleine accused Leroy of being a hopeless provincial and Leroy retorted that he couldn't understand why anyone would travel 4,000 miles to drink spoiled grape juice.

Fortunately, our bagels and cheese tasting proved a scene of reconciliation. With a dozen kinds of cheese and a variety of bagels from which to choose, everybody found something to suit their pleasure.

Melvin and Claire jogged in and praised our protein-rich spread as they made a beeline for the wheat 'n honey bagels and Cheddar. Madeleine chirped paeans to *Brie au bagelettes* while Joe proclaimed this a vintage year for Roquefort on pumpernickel rounds. Hal and Elaine sampled bagels and Brick, Monterey Jack, Jarlsberg and Provolone before they concluded that the bagel's ring shape promotes celestial bliss in any combination. Only Leroy seemed a bit puzzled by it all—he said he'd have to ask his therapist why Limburger and onion bagels make him feel just as happy as cookies and milk.

We were relieved to discover that it wasn't our company but the pretzels and beer that had gone stale. So now we're prepared for all kinds of entertainment—with bagels and cheese fondues, soups, spreads, soufflés and casseroles. We even have a bagel and cheese dessert that Madeleine might call *"un gâteau de fromage"* and Leroy can savor as "creamy comfort cake" but which we recommend simply as "A Cheesecake You'll Cherish!"

"I simply can't resist its chewy good karma!"

The Big Cheese

TRIPLE HEADER

Combine whipped cream cheese and blue cheese; spread on bagel. Top with slice of sharp Cheddar cheese. Broil until bubbly; sprinkle with paprika.

BRIE GRAPEVINE

Spread bagel with Brie cheese. Cut green seedless grapes in half; place cut-sides down on cheese. Garnish with watercress.

A FINE FETA

Brush toasted bagel (garlic) with olive oil. Top with crumbled feta cheese, chopped tomato and onion and sliced black olives.

MUENSTER MELT

Top toasted bagel with slice of Muenster cheese and tomato; sprinkle with minced coriander leaves. Add second slice of cheese; broil until bubbly, about 1 minute.

BRANDIED BLUE

Combine whipped cream cheese, blue cheese and small amount of brandy; spread on bagel (egg). Sprinkle with chopped walnuts.

A SALMON HOOKED ON CHEESE

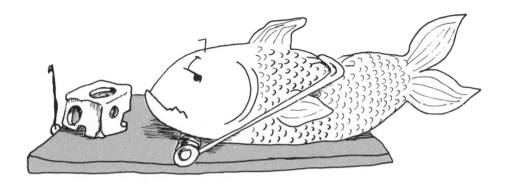

2 tablespoons finely chopped onion
1 rib celery, finely chopped
¼ cup butter or margarine
1 tablespoon flour
1¾ cups milk
2 bagels *(onion),* cut into 1-inch cubes
¼ teaspoon dried thyme leaves
¼ teaspoon salt
⅛ teaspoon pepper
1 can (4 ounces) sliced mushrooms,
    drained
1 can (15 ounces) salmon, drained,
    bones removed
1 cup shredded Cheddar cheese
1 cup shredded Swiss cheese
1 cup shredded Mozzarella cheese
¼ cup finely chopped parsley

1. Heat oven to 350° F. Saute onion and celery in butter in medium saucepan until onion is soft, about 3 minutes. Stir in flour; cook 2 minutes, stirring constantly. Stir in milk; heat to boiling. Cook over medium heat, stirring constantly, until mixture thickens, about 5 minutes.

2. Process bagels in blender or food processor to make fine crumbs. Stir crumbs and remaining ingredients, except parsley, into milk mixture. Spoon mixture into greased baking pan, 11 × 7 inches.

3. Bake covered with aluminum foil 30 minutes. Uncover; bake 30 minutes. Cool 5 minutes. Sprinkle with parsley; cut into squares to serve.

6 servings

NACHO BAGEL FONDUE

　1 medium onion, finely chopped
　1 medium green pepper, finely chopped
¼ cup vegetable oil
¾ cup milk
½ teaspoon paprika
¼ teaspoon ground cumin
¾ teaspoon salt
⅛ teaspoon pepper
　1 teaspoon chili powder
12 ounces shredded sharp Cheddar
　　cheese
　6 bagels, cut into 1-inch pieces, toasted

1. Saute onion and green pepper in oil until onion is tender, about 5
minutes. Stir in milk, paprika, cumin, salt, pepper and chili powder;
reduce heat to low. Stir in cheese; cook, stirring constantly, until cheese
is melted.

2. Pour mixture into fondue pot; keep warm over low flame. Serve toasted
bagels as dippers.

2 cups

LOX 'N CREAM CHEESE FONDUE

3 tablespoons butter or margarine
1 package (8 ounces) cream cheese, cut
    into ½-inch cubes
¼ cup milk
3 ounces lox, cut into ½-inch pieces
1 tablespoon chopped chives
2 teaspoons horseradish
¼ teaspoon salt
⅛ teaspoon white pepper
2 dashes red pepper sauce
6 bagels *(rye),* cut into 1-inch cubes,
    toasted

1. Melt butter over low heat in small saucepan. Add cream cheese and milk; cook, stirring constantly, until cheese is melted. Stir in remaining ingredients except bagels.

2. Pour mixture into fondue pot; keep warm over low flame. Serve bagels as dippers.

2 cups

"SHERRY AMOUR" FONDUE

1 clove garlic, minced
2 tablespoons butter or margarine
½ cup dry sherry
8 ounces shredded Cheddar cheese
½ package (8 ounce size) cream cheese,
    cut into ½-inch cubes
½ teaspoon paprika
6 bagels, cut into 1-inch pieces, toasted
  Vegetable relishes

1. Saute garlic in butter in small saucepan until light brown, about 30 seconds. Stir in sherry; reduce heat to low. Stir in remaining ingredients except bagels and vegetables; cook, stirring constantly, until cheeses are melted.

2. Pour mixture into fondue pot; keep warm over low flame. Serve bagels and vegetables as dippers.

2½ cups

BEER 'N BAGELS SOUP

2 bagels, cut into 1-inch pieces
1 can (12 ounces) beer
2 tablespoons butter or margarine
2 tablespoons flour
3 cups milk
2 tablespoons sugar
½ teaspoon caraway seeds
¼ teaspoon ground ginger
¼ teaspoon salt
1 cup shredded Swiss cheese

1. Process bagel pieces in blender or food processor to make coarse crumbs. Pour beer over crumbs in small bowl; let stand 30 minutes.

2. Melt butter in large saucepan; stir in flour. Cook over medium heat, stirring occasionally, 3 minutes. Stir in milk, sugar, caraway, ginger and salt. Heat to boiling; simmer uncovered 5 minutes, stirring constantly. Stir bagel mixture into soup; cook 5 minutes.

3. Place Swiss cheese in bottoms of 4 soup bowls; pour soup over cheese. Serve immediately.

4 servings

CHED-O-NUT SPREAD

1½ cups shredded Cheddar cheese
½ cup butter or margarine, room temperature
1 cup walnuts or pecans
½ teaspoon Worcestershire sauce
2 to 3 tablespoons dry sherry
12 bagelettes, toasted

1. Process cheese and margarine in blender or food processor until smooth. Add walnuts; process until walnuts are finely chopped. Add Worcestershire and enough sherry for desired consistency.

2. Spoon spread into bowl. Serve with bagelettes.

2½ cups

CHEDDAR CHOWDER

1 carrot, finely chopped
1 rib celery, finely chopped
¼ cup butter or margarine
1 small onion, finely chopped
2 tablespoons flour
3 cups milk
2 cups chicken broth
1 can (17 ounces) whole kernel corn,
    drained
1 can (17 ounces) cream style corn
12 ounces shredded sharp Cheddar
    cheese
1 teaspoon chili powder
½ teaspoon paprika
½ teaspoon salt
¼ teaspoon white pepper
6 bagels
  Butter or margarine
  Chili powder

1. Saute carrot and celery in ¼ cup butter in large saucepan 3 minutes. Add onion; saute 2 minutes. Stir in flour; cook over low heat, stirring constantly, 2 minutes. Stir in milk and chicken broth; simmer uncovered 10 minutes, stirring frequently.

2. Stir in corn, cheese, 1 teaspoon chili powder, the paprika, salt and pepper. Simmer uncovered 5 minutes, stirring occasionally.

3. While soup is cooking, heat oven to broil. Spread bagels with butter; sprinkle with chili powder. Broil until brown, about 1 minute.

4. Serve soup in bowls with toasted bagels.

6 servings

SWISS ONION SOUP-REME!

3 pounds yellow onions, thinly sliced
1 large clove garlic, minced
3 tablespoons butter or margarine
3 tablespoons olive oil
¼ cup all-purpose flour
2 quarts beef broth
1½ cups dry white wine
    Pinch dried thyme leaves
¾ teaspoon salt
¼ teaspoon white pepper
6 ounces shredded Swiss cheese
3 bagels, toasted

1. Saute onions and garlic in butter and olive oil in Dutch oven until onions are golden, about 30 minutes. Stir in flour; cook 5 minutes, stirring occasionally. Stir in broth, wine, thyme, salt and pepper; heat to boiling. Simmer uncovered over low heat until soup has thickened to desired consistency, about 1 hour.

2. Heat oven to broil. Stir half the cheese into the soup; ladle soup into individual oven-proof tureens. Place bagel half on soup in each tureen; sprinkle with remaining cheese.

3. Broil until cheese is melted; about 2 minutes. Serve immediately.

6 servings

GARLIC GALOR-IOUS SPREAD

1 package (8 ounces) cream cheese,
    room temperature
½ cup butter or margarine, room
    temperature
1 large clove garlic, minced
¼ teaspoon Worcestershire sauce
2 drops red pepper sauce
2 to 3 tablespoons dry sherry
12 bagelettes, toasted

1. Process cream cheese and butter in blender or food processor until
   smooth. Add garlic, Worcestershire, red pepper sauce and enough sherry
   for desired consistency.

2. Spoon spread into bowl. Serve with bagelettes.

2 cups

BAGELETTES BRAVISSIMO!

1 package (8 ounces) cream cheese,
    room temperature
4 ounces blue cheese, crumbled
¼ cup Italian salad dressing
¼ cup grated Parmesan cheese
¼ pound Genoa salami, cut into ½-inch
    pieces
12 bagelettes *(onion),* toasted

1. Process all ingredients except bagelettes in blender or food processor
   until smooth.

2. Spoon dip into bowl; serve with bagelettes.

2 cups

PEACHES 'N CREAM SOUFFLÉS

1 package (3 ounces) cream cheese,
    room temperature
½ cup small curd cottage cheese
2 teaspoons lemon juice
2 tablespoons sugar
¼ teaspoon vanilla
    Pinch ground nutmeg
    Pinch ground cloves
2 bagels *(wheat 'n honey),* toasted
8 fresh or canned, drained peach slices

1. Heat oven to broil. Beat cheeses, lemon juice, sugar, vanilla, nutmeg and cloves until fluffy. Spread mixture on bagel halves.

2. Broil bagels 4 inches from heat source until puffed and golden, about 30 seconds. Top each with 2 peach slices.

4 servings

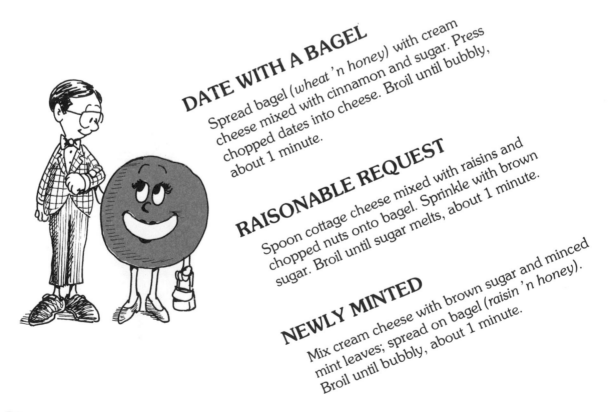

DATE WITH A BAGEL

Spread bagel *(wheat 'n honey)* with cream cheese mixed with cinnamon and sugar. Press chopped dates into cheese. Broil until bubbly, about 1 minute.

RAISONABLE REQUEST

Spoon cottage cheese mixed with raisins and chopped nuts onto bagel. Sprinkle with brown sugar. Broil until sugar melts, about 1 minute.

NEWLY MINTED

Mix cream cheese with brown sugar and minced mint leaves; spread on bagel *(raisin 'n honey).* Broil until bubbly, about 1 minute.

A CHEESECAKE YOU'LL CHERISH!

2 bagels, cut into 1-inch pieces
¼ cup melted butter or margarine
¼ cup sugar
3 packages (8 ounces each) cream
    cheese, room temperature
1¼ cups sugar
2 tablespoons flour
¾ cup sour cream
2 teaspoons vanilla
2 egg yolks
½ cup whipping cream, whipped
2 egg whites, beaten to stiff peaks

1. Heat oven to 325° F. Process bagel pieces in blender or food processor
to make fine crumbs. Mix crumbs, melted butter and ¼ cup sugar; press
mixture evenly on bottom and 1 inch up side of generously buttered
9-inch springform pan. Bake 10 minutes. Cool.

2. Beat cream cheese and 1¼ cups sugar in mixer bowl until fluffy. Beat in
flour, sour cream, vanilla and egg yolks. Fold whipped cream into
mixture; fold egg whites into mixture. Spoon mixture into crust.

3. Bake 1½ hours. Cool 1 hour on wire rack. Serve warm or refrigerate and
serve chilled.

16 servings

The Snack Knack

Only a Very Worthy Cause could prompt us to set aside our bagels long enough to sound a clarion for justice. We don't willingly suffer many such distractions, but we do feel that the prevailing mood in this country demands some immediate action.

The cause we espouse is that of snackers, nibblers and noshers (call them what you will!). These are the people who quake with fear when admonished to "avoid eating between meals," the people to whom "three squares a day" represent a state of hardship.

Slandered as slovenly, crumb-trailing boors, snackers are too often depicted in the media as bumbling Dagwood Bumsteads. You never see Superman unwrapping a candy bar in mid-air or James Bond dashing the last sips of his milkshake in the enemy's face. Indeed, the whole country may crunch attentively when the President addresses them on television; yet you never see America's leader reach for anything but a glass of water during prime time.

But who, we ask, are the silent majority if not those of us who tiptoe to the refrigerator in the dead of night? Who maintains the tradition of resourcefulness and ingenuity if not those who seize sustenance from half a can of sardines, a nibble of cheese and a bagelette? Who exemplifies courage if not we who retire without trepidation after a bedtime snack of pastrami and spaghetti sauce on a bagel?

Surely the stereotype of the snacker is unfair. Nobody clever enough to quell hunger with liverwurst and guacamole on a bagel can be accused of narrow-minded ignorance. Nor should those who dutifully collect leftover morsels and stray dabs of sauces on neat rounds of bagel be labeled unkempt. And no image could be more untrue than that of us nibblers as lazy and weak—when everyone knows how much time and energy we devote to our calling!

So there! We rest our case in order to return to the business at hand—a snacklover's tribute to a freezer full of bagels. Our donations to what we consider a Very Worthy Cause include bowlfuls of toothsome munching, tubs of soul-salving dips and a pantry's worth of hit-the-spot combos.

"You didn't happen to see the face cream I keep in the refrigerator, did you?"

POP GOES THE BAGEL

2 bagels *(egg)*
4 cups popped corn
2 cups wheat chex cereal
1 cup cashews
4 tablespoons butter or margarine, melted
1 teaspoon dried oregano leaves
½ teaspoon dried basil leaves
¼ teaspoon garlic powder
¼ cup dried parsley flakes
1 cup grated Parmesan cheese

1. Heat oven to 250°F. Slice bagels thinly by hand or in food processor. Mix bagel slices, popped corn, cereal and cashews in large bowl. Mix butter and remaining ingredients except parsley and cheese; pour over corn mixture and mix well. Spread mixture on ungreased cookie sheet.

2. Bake 1 hour, stirring every 10 minutes. Cool; mix in parsley and cheese. Store in airtight container.

About 8 cups

NIBBLER'S NIRVANA

2 bagels
2 cups toasted wheat cereal
1 cup wheat chex cereal
2 cups corn chex cereal
2 cups corn chips
1 cup pecans
4 tablespoons butter or margarine, melted
2 teaspoons Worcestershire sauce
1 tablespoon spicy brown mustard
2 tablespoons soy sauce
½ teaspoon garlic powder
½ teaspoon onion salt

1. Heat oven to 250°F. Slice bagels thinly by hand or in food processor. Mix bagel slices, cereals, corn chips and pecans in large bowl. Mix butter and remaining ingredients; pour over cereal mixture and mix well. Spread mixture on ungreased cookie sheet.

2. Bake 1 hour, stirring every 10 minutes. Cool; store in airtight container.

About 8 cups

MAPLE BAGOLA

2 bagels *(wheat 'n honey)*, cut into ½-inch
   pieces
   1 cup uncooked rolled oats
   ½ cup shredded coconut
   ½ cup wheat germ
   1 teaspoon ground cinnamon
   ¼ teaspoon ground nutmeg
   ½ cup honey
   ½ cup maple syrup
   1 cup golden raisins
   1 cup mixed dried fruit, cut into ½-inch
   pieces

1. Heat oven to 250° F. Mix bagel pieces, oats, coconut and wheat germ
   in large bowl. Sprinkle with cinnamon and nutmeg; toss lightly. Pour
   honey and syrup over mixture; mix well and spread evenly on
   ungreased cookie sheet.

2. Bake 60 minutes, stirring every 10 minutes. Cool. Transfer mixture to
   large bowl; mix in raisins and dried fruit. Store in airtight container.

About 6 cups

CRAZY MIXED UP NUTS

2 bagels, cut into ½-inch pieces
½ cup wheat germ
1 cup sunflower nuts
1 cup peanuts
1 cup pecans
1 cup cashews
½ teaspoon curry powder
½ teaspoon ground cumin
½ cup melted butter or margarine

1. Heat oven to 250°F. Mix bagel pieces, wheat germ, sunflower nuts,
   peanuts, pecans and cashews in large bowl. Stir curry and cumin into
   butter; pour over nut mixture. Mix well and spread evenly on ungreased
   cookie sheet.

2. Bake 60 minutes, stirring every 10 minutes. Cool. Store in airtight
   container.

About 6 cups

'Fridge-Raiders' Rations

FRUIT 'N NOSH

Spread bagel (*wheat 'n honey*) with peanut butter mixed with a generous pinch of curry powder and raisins. Sprinkle with shredded coconut.

SARDINE CATCH

Mix cream cheese with horseradish; spread on bagel. Top with sardines; sprinkle with chopped green onion.

SALAAMI, SALAMI

Top buttered bagel (*onion*) with slices of salami. Sprinkle with shredded Muenster cheese and green olive slices. Broil until bubbly.

TINGLY BLISS

Butter bagel halves; spread with mustard. Top with slices of radish; sprinkle with seasoned salt.

QUICK CRUNCH

Combine cream cheese with crumbled blue cheese. Spread on bagel. Top with celery slices; sprinkle with paprika.

CLAMDIGGER'S CACHE

 1 cup cottage cheese
¼ cup whipped cream cheese
 1 can (6½ ounces) chopped clams,
     drained
 3 tablespoons minced chives
½ teaspoon lemon juice
¼ teaspoon salt
⅛ teaspoon pepper
 4 bagels *(rye)* cut into 1-inch pieces
     toasted

1. Mix all ingredients except bagels in small bowl. Refrigerate covered several hours for flavors to blend.

2. Spoon dip into bowl. Serve chilled with bagels for dippers.

About 1¾ cups

HERRING TAKES A DIP

 1 jar (8 ounces) herring in wine sauce,
     undrained
 1 cup cottage cheese
½ cup sour cream
¼ cup minced parsley
 1 tablespoon horseradish
⅛ teaspoon pepper
12 bagelettes, cut into quarters, toasted

1. Process all ingredients except bagelettes in blender or food processor until smooth. Refrigerate covered several hours for flavors to blend.

2. Spoon dip into bowl. Serve chilled with bagelettes for dippers.

About 2 cups

SERENDIPITY-DIPITY

4 ounces shredded sharp Cheddar
    cheese
½ package (8-ounce size) cream cheese,
    room temperature
½ cup applesauce
¼ cup pecans
½ teaspoon Worcestershire sauce
¼ teaspoon curry powder
4 bagels, cut into 1-inch pieces, toasted

1. Process all ingredients except bagels in blender or food processor until smooth. Refrigerate covered several hours for flavors to blend.

2. Spoon dip into bowl. Serve at room temperature with bagel pieces for dippers.

About 1½ cups

DUTCH TREAT

8 ounces smoked Edam cheese, cut into
    1-inch cubes
½ cup whipping cream
1 clove garlic, minced
1 teaspoon Dijon-style mustard
1 teaspoon chopped chives
4 slices bacon, cooked crisp, crumbled
4 bagels, cut into 1-inch pieces,
    toasted

1. Process all ingredients except bacon and bagels in blender or food processor until smooth. Stir in bacon. Refrigerate covered several hours for flavors to blend.

2. Spoon dip into bowl. Serve at room temperature with bagel pieces for dippers.

About 1¼ cups

How Sweet It Is!

The gastronomic world seems to be divided into two camps.

There are those who automatically murmur "Just coffee, please," whenever a restaurant waiter asks them if they would care for dessert. Or those who pat their (invariably flat) stomachs and reply, "None for me, thank you."

And then there are the rest of us: We who read every menu backwards and would gladly order strawberry shortcake as an appetizer—if no one were watching! We who look furtively around the table to see if somebody else will share the chocolate mousse with us so that we can reciprocate with the cherry pie. We who could devour a seven-course dinner and still feel cheated if the dessert were plain fruit. We who remain unconvinced that whipped cream isn't as good an antidote to stress as any other.

We have noticed significant differences between Us and Them. For one thing, we operate on the "leave room" principle and they don't. Which is to say, we never accept a second portion of vegetables and we are careful not to drink too much water with meals—so as always to leave room for more important matters.

Another thing we've come to realize is that we dress differently. They tend to sport well-fitted fashions, while we have learned to anticipate the meal-end choice between seam splits and banana splits by wearing loose clothing. Which also makes us look like we've recently shed a pound or two and frees us from the disapproving glances of the "just coffee" crew.

Dessert detractors always seem to think that their show of will power demonstrates greater strength on their side. We disagree. Not only do we have the infinite realm of sweet dreams on our side but also the power of bagels. And you can sample the efficacy of this arsenal for yourself—in every cinnamon-scented forkful of Bagel Apple Tart and every chocolaty bite of Bagels Hélène, in every creamy morsel of Bagel Bavarian and every crisp, honey-drenched triangle of Bagel Baklava. To say nothing of the Bagel Babas, Bread Pudding, Danish. . . .and more!

BAGEL BAVARIAN

2 packages (10 ounces each) frozen
   raspberries, thawed
¼ cup sugar
2 tablespoons orange-flavor liqueur
1 envelope unflavored gelatin
3 egg yolks
½ cup milk
3 bagelettes
¼ cup orange-flavor liqueur
3 egg whites
¾ cup whipping cream

1. Process raspberries in blender or food processor until smooth. Add sugar
and 2 tablespoons liqueur; process several seconds to mix. Pour half the
raspberry mixture into small saucepan; refrigerate remaining raspberry
mixture. Stir gelatin into saucepan; cook over low heat, stirring
constantly, until gelatin is melted, about 3 minutes. Cool to room
temperature.

2. Beat egg yolks until thick and lemon colored, about 5 minutes. Beat milk
into egg yolks gradually; stir egg mixture into cooled raspberries. Cook
over low heat, stirring constantly, until mixture begins to thicken, about
5 minutes. Refrigerate until mixture mounds on a spoon, about 30
minutes.

3. Slice bagelettes in food processor, or slice thinly by hand. Sprinkle slices
with ¼ cup liqueur. Press slices on bottom and side of generously
buttered 1½-quart mold or souffle dish.

4. Beat egg whites in medium mixer bowl until stiff but not dry peaks form.
In separate bowl, beat whipping cream to stiff peaks. Fold egg whites and
whipping cream into raspberry-gelatin mixture; pour into mold.
Refrigerate until firm, 4 to 6 hours.

5. Loosen top edge of mold with knife; dip mold briefly into warm water.
Unmold on serving plate. Cut into wedges; serve with remaining
raspberry sauce.

8 to 10 servings

BAGEL BREAD PUDDING

3 large eggs
½ cup sugar
¼ cup honey
2 cups milk
½ cup light cream
¼ cup rum
1 teaspoon vanilla

¾ teaspoon ground cinnamon
¼ teaspoon ground cardamom
4 bagels *(raisin 'n honey)*, cut into ½-inch pieces
½ cup raisins
1 cup chopped pecans or almonds

1. Beat eggs, sugar and honey in small mixer bowl until smooth. Mix in milk, cream, rum, vanilla, cinnamon and cardamom. Pour mixture over bagels, raisins and nuts in large bowl; mix well. Let stand 1 hour; stir frequently.

2. Heat oven to 350° F. Spoon pudding into buttered 2-quart casserole. Bake covered 30 minutes. Uncover; bake 30 minutes. Serve warm, or refrigerate and serve cold.

8 servings

BAGEL BABAS

4 bagels *(egg)*
½ cup water
½ cup sugar
¼ cup dark rum
⅓ cup whipping cream
½ teaspoon vanilla
2 teaspoons sugar
2 tablespoons sour cream

1. Place bagels, cut-sides up, in baking pan. Pierce bagels liberally with tines of fork.

2. Heat water, ½ cup sugar and the rum to boiling; reduce heat. Simmer uncovered 5 minutes. Spoon hot syrup over bagels. Let stand 5 minutes.

3. Beat whipping cream, vanilla and 2 teaspoons sugar in small mixer bowl until stiff peaks form. Mix in sour cream.

4. Place bagels on serving plates; top with dollops of whipped cream.

8 servings

BAGEL DANISH

2 packages (3 ounces each) cream cheese, room temperature
2 teaspoons sugar
½ teaspoon grated orange rind

6 bagels, toasted
1 cup powdered sugar
2 to 3 tablespoons orange juice
3 tablespoons chopped pecans

1. Beat cream cheese in small mixer bowl until fluffy. Mix in sugar and orange rind. Spread mixture on bottom halves of bagels; cover with top halves.

2. Mix powdered sugar with enough orange juice to make thin, pourable frosting. Drizzle frosting over tops of bagels. Sprinkle with pecans.

6 servings

ALOHA FONDUE

2 tablespoons butter or margarine
2 packages (8 ounces each) cream cheese
¼ cup milk
3 tablespoons lemon juice
2 tablespoons honey
2 tablespoons brandy
1 can (8 ounces) crushed pineapple, undrained
4 bagels, buttered
  Sugar
  Ground cinnamon
  Assorted fruit, cut into 1-inch pieces

1. Melt butter in medium saucepan; add cream cheese. Cook over low heat, stirring constantly, until cheese is melted, about 5 minutes. Stir in milk, lemon juice, honey, brandy and pineapple. Cook over medium heat, stirring occasionally, until hot through, about 5 minutes.

2. Sprinkle bagels with sugar and cinnamon; broil until toasted, about 1 minute. Cool slightly; cut into 1-inch pieces.

3. Keep fondue warm in chafing dish or fondue pot. Serve bagels and fruit as dippers.

3½ cups

BAGEL BAKLAVA

2 bagels *(wheat 'n honey),* cut into 1-inch
    pieces
1 cup walnuts
½ cup almonds
½ cup water
½ cup sugar
¼ cup honey
⅛ teaspoon ground cloves
⅛ teaspoon ground cinnamon
1 piece lemon rind (1 inch)
1 egg
1 pound fillo pastry
½ pound melted butter or margarine

1. Process bagels, walnuts and almonds in blender or food processor until finely ground.

2. Heat water, sugar, honey, cloves, cinnamon and lemon rind in small saucepan to boiling; reduce heat. Simmer uncovered 15 minutes; cool 5 minutes. Remove lemon rind. Mix syrup into bagel mixture in medium bowl; mix in egg.

3. Cut fillo pastry in half lengthwise; place under damp towels to prevent drying. Brush 1 piece fillo with melted butter; fold in half lengthwise and brush with butter again. Place 1 tablespoon bagel mixture on lower corner; fold bottom edge to form triangle. Continue folding, like a flag, to top of pastry; place on ungreased cookie sheet. Repeat with remaining fillo and bagel mixture. Brush tops of pastries with butter.

4. Heat oven to 325° F. Bake until pastries are golden, 30 to 35 minutes. Cool on wire rack.

36 pastries

BAGEL NOTE: Pastries can be wrapped in aluminum foil and frozen. Heat frozen pastries at 325° F. until hot, about 20 minutes.

91

BAGEL SWEET-TART CRUST

2 bagels, cut into ½-inch pieces
1 hard-cooked egg, cut into wedges
⅓ cup butter or margarine, melted
¼ cup sugar
1 egg yolk

1. Heat oven to 325° F. Process bagel pieces in blender or food processor to make coarse crumbs; spread on cookie sheet. Bake until toasted, about 15 minutes, stirring occasionally.

2. Process bagel crumbs and hard-cooked egg in blender or food processor until finely ground; mix in butter, sugar and egg yolk. Press mixture on bottom and side of ungreased 9-inch tart pan.

3. Bake until golden and firm, about 20 minutes. Cool on wire rack. Fill as desired, using recipes below.

1 nine-inch crust

SPICED APPLE FILLING

4 medium apples, peeled, cored, thinly
　　sliced
¼ cup sugar
½ teaspoon ground cinnamon
⅛ teaspoon ground cloves
¼ cup apple jelly

1. Heat oven to 400 ° F. Toss apples with sugar, cinnamon and cloves in large bowl; arrange slices attractively in baked tart crust. Bake until apples are tender and light brown, about 40 minutes. Cool on wire rack.

2. Heat jelly in small saucepan until melted; brush on apples.

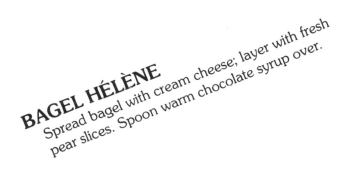

BAGEL HÉLÈNE
Spread bagel with cream cheese; layer with fresh pear slices. Spoon warm chocolate syrup over.

PINEAPPLE-CHEESE FILLING

1 package (8 ounces) cream cheese,
  room temperature
1 tablespoon sugar
1 tablespoon milk
1 teaspoon vanilla
1 medium pineapple
½ cup apple jelly

1. Beat cream cheese, sugar, milk and vanilla in small mixer bowl until fluffy. Spread mixture in bottom of baked tart crust.

2. Slice rind from pineapple; cut out eyes. Slice pineapple in half lengthwise; cut into ½-inch slices. Remove core from slices; cut slices into chunks. Arrange pineapple attractively on cream cheese.

3. Heat jelly in small saucepan until melted; brush on pineapple.

CHERRY FILLING

1 can (16 ounces) cherry pie filling
1 to 2 tablespoons lemon juice
2 teaspoons grated lemon rind
½ teaspoon ground cinnamon
¼ teaspoon ground nutmeg

1. Mix all ingredients, using enough lemon juice for desired flavor. Spoon filling into baked tart crust.

GINGER PEACHY
Sprinkle bagel with orange-flavor liqueur; top with fresh peach slices. Top with crushed ginger snaps and a dash of cinnamon.

TOP BANANA
Spread toasted bagel (egg) with sour cream; sprinkle generously with chopped peanuts. Layer with banana slices; garnish with dollop of sour cream and dash of nutmeg.

The Shape-up, Stay-fit Bagel

Just because bagels are round and chubby doesn't mean you have to be. Our special Bageleaters-Are-Beautiful program is designed to keep you as firm as a bagel but much more shapely.

Before you embark on our program, you must develop the right mental attitude. If you don't think of yourself as a Thin Gorgeous Person, you won't become one. How do you cultivate this frame of mind if your stomach only allows you to think on "full" and your thighs lapsed long, long ago? Well, you should take it a step at a time—and we mean that literally. One of the best things you can do is walk rather than drive to the supermarket; a half hour of vigorous walking will burn off at least one bagel—or 150 calories. If you run to the store, you will burn off two bagels. (And if you swim across a lake to get there, you can consume a whole bagful and nobody will know the difference.)

Once you've begun to think of yourself as a Thin Gorgeous Person, glamour is practically at your doorstep. And we all know what glamorous people do—they put on slinky exercise outfits and work out in gyms. We work out with bagels. Here is our regimen.

Bagel Jacks Stand erect with a bagel clutched in each hand. Jump up, spread feet apart to shoulder-width, and clap the bagels together overhead. Return to original position. Repeat 20 times.

Bagel Toes Stand with feet together and a bagel in each hand. Reach down and place the bagels on your toes. Stand up straight; then reach down (yes, without bending your knees!) and touch the bagels. Slowly stand up straight again. Repeat 10 times.

Bagel Twists Lie flat on your back with your arms out to the sides and a bagel clutched between your feet. Keeping your legs straight, and without dropping the bagel, raise your legs until they are perpendicular to your body. Lower legs to the left, raise them up again, and then lower them to the right. Repeat 15 times.

Bagel Lifts Lie flat on your back with your arms out to the sides and a bagel clutched between your feet. Very slowly raise your legs to a 45 degree angle and hold for a count of ten. (You forgot you had that muscle, right?) Then very slowly lower your legs to the floor. Repeat 12 times.

It always seems like glamorous people subsist on things like pomegranate seeds and mineral water. But it's not true—nobody can live on pomegranate seeds and work out in slinky gym clothes at the same time. Thin Gorgeous Persons eat bagels, feel terrific, and love every calorie-counted bite!

BAGELEATERS-ARE-BEAUTIFUL DIET TACTICS

We have tried all kinds of diets: the High-Energy Carob Bar and Hay Seed Diet; Dr. Snapoutofit's Special Mildew Diet; Hokey Lopez's Tequilla and Banana Diet; Sophie Slender's Liquid Love Diet—the whole works! Although some of these did offer some attractive side effects, we didn't lose much weight on them. So we have returned to straight calorie counting. And we count bagels among our favorite calories!

Most bagels have 150 calories each; some flavors have about 10 calories more (check the nutrition information on the package). Bagelettes have 75 calories.

Here are some ways we've discovered that will make our bagel calories go further:

Bagel Slices Cut each bagel half in half horizontally; each skinny slice has about 37 calories—fewer than a slice of bread. You can use these slices for sandwiches or as a base for broiled meats. Bagels sliced paper thin in a food processor or by hand make a great snack or a lower-calorie base for dishes usually served over rice, noodles or spaghetti; sprinkle these "chips" with seasoned, garlic, onion or celery salt and toast them in the oven.

Lo-Cal Butter No matter how you slice your bagel, you can spread it with fewer calories by whipping up some lo-cal butter or margarine. Beat ½ cup softened butter or margarine until fluffy; gradually beat in ½ cup water. Mix in any kind of herb or spice. Refrigerate until spreadable. Each tablespoonful has only 50 calories—half the amount of regular spreads!

Bagel Crumbs Process bagels in a blender or food processor to make crumbs; one bagel yields one cup of crumbs. Sprinkle the crumbs with herbs or cinnamon and nutmeg and toast them in the oven. You can enjoy the satisfying crunchiness of this crumb topping on broiled meats, steamed vegetables, fresh fruit and low-calorie puddings—at only nine calories for each tablespoonful.

Bagel Go-Withs The following chart lists foods that go well with bagels when you're counting calories; you can calculate your own combinations from them. We have counted the calories in each serving of the recipes in this chapter; so you'll encounter no bagel guesswork there either!

Condiments

Barbecue Sauce	1 tablespoon	26
Catsup	1 tablespoon	18
Chili Sauce	1 tablespoon	17
Chutney	1 tablespoon	53
Dill Pickles	1 large	11
Horseradish	1 teaspoon	9
Pickle Relish	1 tablespoon	17
Soy Sauce	1 teaspoon	3
Tomato Sauce	1 tablespoon	6
Yellow Mustard	1 teaspoon	10

Dairy Products

Butter	1 tablespoon	100
Cheese		
American	1 slice	107
Blue	1 tablespoon	49
Cheddar, shredded	1 tablespoon	28
Cottage	¼ cup	60
Cream	1 tablespoon	52
Swiss	1 slice	106
Egg, poached or boiled	1 whole	78
Margarine	1 tablespoon	100
Diet	1 tablespoon	50

Fish

Caviar	1 tablespoon	96
Clams, steamed	2 large	41
Crab, steamed	2 ounces	47
Fish Sticks	2 sticks	110
Herring, pickled	3½ ounces	233
Lobster, steamed	3 ounces	91
Salmon, canned	¼ cup	108
Salmon, smoked	3½ ounces	176
Sardines	4 medium	156
Shrimp, raw	3½ ounces	91
Tuna, in oil	¼ cup	78
in water	¼ cup	64

Fruit

Apple	1 medium	75
Applesauce	½ cup	115
Banana	1 small	85
Blueberries	½ cup	42
Cherries	½ cup	40
Dates, dry, pitted	¼ cup	122
Grapefruit	½ medium	41
Nectarines	1 medium	32
Oranges	1 medium	73
Peaches	1 medium	38
Pears	1 medium	122
Pineapple, chunks	½ cup	34
crushed	½ cup	50
Prunes, pitted	¼ cup	125
Raisins	¼ cup	103
Raspberries	½ cup	42
Strawberries	5 medium	18

Meat and Poultry

Beef, roasted, lean	3 ounces	165
Dried chipped	2 slices	57
Hamburger, broiled	1 medium	248
Chicken, roasted	3½ ounces	200
Livers	2 medium	144
Corned Beef Hash	3 ounces	185
Lamb, roasted	3½ ounces	242
Lunchmeat		
Bologna	1 slice	66
Hot Dog	1	124
Liver Sausage	1 slice	79
Pork, roasted	3½ ounces	239
Bacon	1 slice	50
Ham	3 ounces	360
Sausage	2 links	160

Vegetables

Avocado	¼ cup mashed	76
Artichokes	1 medium	44
Asparagus	3½ ounces	26
Beans, Green	½ cup	16
Kidney	¼ cup	56
Bean Sprouts	½ cup	23
Beets, canned	½ cup	18
Broccoli	3½ ounces	26
Cabbage, shredded	½ cup	13
Carrots	1 small	21
Cauliflower	½ cup	14
Celery	1 rib	10
Cucumber	½ medium	8
Eggplant	½ cup	19
Lentils	¼ cup	40
Lettuce, shredded	½ cup	9
Mushrooms	2 large	14
Onion, Yellow	1 small	38
Green	2 medium	18
Peas, canned	¼ cup	20
Peppers, green	1 large	22
Radishes	5 small	9
Spinach, raw	1 cup	26
Tomatoes	1 small	22

SLIM FISHIN'

1 bagel, cut into ½-inch pieces
½ teaspoon paprika
½ teaspoon onion salt
½ teaspoon salt
¼ teaspoon pepper

1 pound frozen fish fillets (cod, halibut or haddock), thawed
½ cup buttermilk
1 tablespoon diet margarine
4 lemon wedges

1. Heat oven to 425° F. Process bagel in blender or food processor to make fine crumbs; mix with paprika, onion salt, salt and pepper in shallow bowl.

2. Dip fish into buttermilk; coat with crumb mixture. Arrange fish in baking pan coated with 1 tablespoon margarine. Bake uncovered until fish is tender and flakes with a fork, about 25 minutes. Serve with lemon wedges.

4 servings
(about 150 calories each)

CALORIE-CLEVER CHICKEN

2 bagels
½ teaspoon onion salt
¼ teaspoon garlic powder
1 pound boned, skinned chicken breast
¼ teaspoon salt
⅛ teaspoon pepper

¼ teaspoon garlic powder
1 medium onion, coarsely chopped
3 tablespoons diet margarine
½ cup chopped green pepper
2 medium tomatoes, coarsely chopped

1. Heat oven to 400° F. Slice bagels in food processor or slice thinly by hand. Sprinkle bagels with onion salt and ¼ teaspoon garlic powder. Bake on cookie sheet until golden, about 5 minutes on each side.

2. Sprinkle chicken with salt, pepper and ¼ teaspoon garlic powder; cut into ¼-inch strips. Saute onion in margarine in large skillet 3 minutes. Stir in green pepper and tomatoes; cook over medium heat 2 minutes. Add chicken; cook, stirring frequently, until chicken is cooked and tender, about 5 minutes.

3. Arrange bagel slices on plates; spoon chicken mixture over.

4 servings
(about 240 calories each)

FRUIT BAGATELLE

¾ cup low-fat cottage cheese with
    pineapple
¼ cup plain low-fat yogurt
1 teaspoon dried mint leaves
1 teaspoon lemon juice
1 medium orange, peeled, cut into
    segments
1 medium apple, cored, cut into 8 wedges

1 medium pear, cored, cut into 8 wedges
1 large banana, sliced
12 large strawberries, cut in half
    Mint or parsley sprigs
¼ cup low-fat cottage cheese with
    pineapple
4 bagelettes, toasted

1. Mix ¾ cup cottage cheese, the yogurt, dried mint and lemon juice.
Refrigerate until serving time.

2. Arrange fruit attractively on serving platter or individual plates; garnish
with mint. Spoon dressing over salad.

3. Spread ¼ cup cottage cheese on bagelettes; serve with salad.

4 servings
(about 260 calories each)

SALAD SATISFACTION

2 bagels *(poppyseed),* cut into ¼-inch
    pieces, toasted
2 cups flaked, cooked fish (cod, halibut or
    haddock)
2 medium potatoes, cooked, pared, thinly
    sliced
1 small cucumber, scored, cut into ½-inch
    cubes
2 tablespoons minced parsley
¼ cup thinly sliced green onions
½ cup chopped green pepper
¾ cup thinly sliced celery

2 tomatoes, quartered, thinly sliced
3 tablespoons safflower oil
2 tablespoons olive oil
2 tablespoons red wine vinegar
2 tablespoons lemon juice
¼ teaspoon dried basil leaves
⅛ teaspoon dried thyme leaves
    Dash red pepper sauce
½ teaspoon salt
¼ teaspoon pepper

1. Toss bagels, fish, potatoes, cucumber, parsley, green onions, green
pepper, celery and tomatoes in large bowl. Mix remaining ingredients;
pour over salad and toss. Refrigerate covered several hours. Let stand at
room temperature 30 minutes; toss before serving.

6 servings
(about 270 calories each)

SLENDER STUFFED ARTICHOKES

2 medium artichokes
1 medium onion, minced
1 clove garlic, minced
2 tablespoons diet margarine
2 plain bagels, cut into ½-inch pieces
1 tablespoon Dijon-style mustard
1 tablespoon lemon juice
2 tablespoons sherry, if desired
1 teaspoon dried dill weed
3 to 4 tablespoons tomato juice
4 thin lemon slices

1. Trim stem from base of artichokes; slice 1 inch off tops. Cut points off leaves with scissors. Stand artichokes in saucepan with 2 inches water; heat to boiling. Simmer covered until tender, 30 to 40 minutes; drain.

2. Saute onion and garlic in margarine in small skillet until onion is tender, about 5 minutes. Process bagel pieces in blender or food processor to make coarse crumbs; stir into skillet. Cook, stirring constantly, until crumbs are browned, about 5 minutes. Stir in mustard, lemon juice, sherry, dill weed and enough tomato juice for mixture to hold together.

3. Gently pull center leaves of artichoke apart; remove choke with spoon. Push bagel stuffing between leaves; twist lemon slices and insert in centers of artichokes.

2 servings
(about 300 calories each)

THINK-THIN PLATTER

½ cup low-calorie Italian salad dressing
½ cup plain low-fat yogurt
½ cup tomato juice
3 small sweet pickles, finely chopped
½ teaspoon paprika
¼ teaspoon celery salt
¼ teaspoon onion salt
2 bagels
½ teaspoon celery salt
7 ounces spinach, torn into bite-size
    pieces
1 medium carrot, shredded
½ cup coarsely chopped green pepper
1 cup cauliflowerets
1 small cucumber, scored, thinly sliced
8 fresh mushrooms, thinly sliced
8 radish roses
4 hard-cooked eggs, cut into wedges
4 ounces sliced roast beef
4 ounces sliced turkey breast
4 ounces Swiss cheese, cut into strips
4 ounces American cheese, cut into strips

1. Mix salad dressing, yogurt, tomato juice, pickles, paprika, ¼ teaspoon celery salt and the onion salt. Refrigerate until serving time.

2. Slice bagels in food processor or slice very thinly by hand; sprinkle with ½ teaspoon celery salt. Broil until toasted on both sides.

3. Arrange remaining ingredients attractively on large serving platter. Pass dressing for salad; serve with bagel slices.

8 servings
(about 290 calories each)

Kids Raid the Bagels

We received this letter the other day from 28 fourth-graders at our local elementary school:

Dear Bagel People,

How come you say so many silly things about bagels? Why don't you discust [sic] what's really important?

We cook a lot and take bagels serialously [sic]. So we want to tell you some things that you may not know about why bagels are exelent [sic].

1. FAST. When you come home from school and are starving, you can put cream cheese or peanut butter on bagels and eat right away.

2. ALWAYS IN FREEZER. Not like cake that someone might have got to first or bread with furry blue mold. Or a rottin [sic] banana that nobody wants.

3. GOOD WITH EVERYTHING. You can even mash the banana and put it on a bagel if there is no cheese or anything.

4. TAKE IT WITH YOU. You can take a bagel on your bike or to a friend's house.

5. TWO HALFS [sic]. You can give your friend half of your bagel if he doesn't have one.

6. FILLS YOU UP.

7. MAKES GOOD PIZZA. Very chewy and substanshul [sic].

8. MAKES VERY GOOD S'MORES. Much better than grame [sic] crackers with marshmallows and chocolate bars. Doesn't crumble and fall apart.

9. STOPS CRYING. You can even give your baby sister a bagel and she will stop crying.

10. HARD BUTTER. Not a big problem with bagels which are strong.

11. VERY GOOD FOR DUNKING. Try them with hot chocolate or cocoa if you haven't already.

12. CAN BE SWEET OR SALTY. Deepends [sic] on what you put on them.

Sincerely yours,
[28 signatures]
Cherry Valley School

Along with their wise advice, the students in Mrs. Bagello's classroom also sent suggestions for recipes, which we have developed and wish to share with you.

102

"I'll throw in two marbles, half a stick of gum and one chance to play with my gerbils . . ."

SUNFLOWER SANDWICHES

¼ cup mayonnaise or salad dressing
2 tablespoons pickle relish
2 teaspoons yellow mustard
2 bagels
8 slices bologna
4 slices American cheese
4 black or green olives

1. Set the oven at 350° F. Mix up the mayonnaise, pickle relish and mustard in a little bowl. Spread some on the bagels; you will have some left over. Put the bagels on a cookie sheet.

2. Cut each slice of bologna into 4 triangle-shaped pieces. Put them on the bagels so that the pieces are overlapping and the pointed ends are on the outside. Cut each slice of cheese into triangle-shaped pieces too. Put the cheese in the middle of the bologna so it looks like a flower. Put a little spoonful of the leftover mayonnaise stuff in the middle of the cheese; stick in an olive.

3. Bake the bagels until they are hot, about 10 minutes. Let them cool for a minute before you gobble them up!

4 servings

MY OWN PIZZAS

4 ounces hamburger or sausage
¾ teaspoon dried oregano leaves
¾ cup tomato sauce
3 bagels *(onion)*
1 cup shredded Mozzarella or Cheddar
   cheese

1. Set the oven at 400° F. Put the hamburger in a skillet; cook it on medium heat until it is all brown and cooked. Stir it once in a while.

2. Mix the oregano into the tomato sauce; spread the sauce on the bagels. Put the meat on the bagels, dividing it as evenly as you can. Sprinkle the cheese on the top. Put the bagels on a cookie sheet.

3. Bake the bagels until the cheese is melted and gets bubbly, about 7 minutes. Let the pizzas cool a little before you eat them because they are really hot!

4 to 6 servings

MAKE-A-FACE SANDWICHES

3 hard-cooked eggs
3 small sweet pickles
⅓ cup mayonnaise or salad dressing
1 tablespoon catsup
1 teaspoon yellow mustard
¼ teaspoon salt
2 bagels (egg)
12 parsley sprigs
4 black olives
1 small sweet pickle
4 strips pimiento

1. Chop up the eggs and 3 sweet pickles and put them in a little bowl. Mix in the mayonnaise, catsup, mustard and salt; stir until everything is mixed really well. Spread the egg salad on the bagels.

2. Decorate the bagels to look like faces. Use the parsley to make the hair. Cut the olives in half and make the eyes. Cut the pickle in strips and make noses and ears. Make smiles (or frowns) with the pimiento.

4 servings

REALLY GREAT HOT DOGS

4 hot dogs
¼ cup catsup
2 tablespoons pickle relish
2 teaspoons yellow mustard
2 bagels
½ cup shredded Cheddar cheese
4 slices tomato
4 parsley sprigs

1. Set the oven at broil. Make 8 diagonal cuts in each hot dog, cutting about halfway through. Put the hot dogs on the broiler pan. Broil them 4 inches from the heat until they turn brown and curl into circles; turn them over and let them turn brown on the other side. This will take about 1 minute on each side.

2. Mix up the catsup, pickle relish and mustard in a little bowl. Spread the stuff on the bagels. Sprinkle on the cheese. Put the bagels on the broiler pan. Broil them 4 inches from the heat until the cheese melts, about 2 minutes.

3. Put a tomato slice on each bagel, then a hot dog. Put a parsley sprig in the middle of each one so they will look pretty. Your mom and dad will like these too!

4 servings

BAGEL SUNDAE
Put a scoop of strawberry ice cream on a bagel (wheat 'n honey). Pour chocolate sauce over the top. Sprinkle the whole thing with chopped nuts. Put on some whipped cream if you have some. And a red cherry!

BEST BURGERS
Mix up some hamburger with some catsup and pickle relish. Spread the hamburger on a bagel. Cook it under the broiler until the meat is cooked and turns brown. Put on some more catsup or mustard, whichever you like better.

BAGEL S'MORES

2 chocolate candy bars
2 bagels *(raisin 'n honey)*
12 marshmallows

1. Set the oven at 375° F. Break the candy bar up into squares; divide the chocolate on the bagels. Put the bagels on a cookie sheet. Put 3 marshmallows on top of the chocolate on each bagel.

2. Bake the bagels until the marshmallows puff up and turn brown. Let them cool a few minutes before you eat them. They are so good you will want s'more, which is how they got their name!

4 servings

FROSTED BANANA BAGELS

1 small banana
½ cup canned vanilla or chocolate frosting
3 bagels
½ cup chopped peanuts

1. Peel the banana and put it in a little bowl; mash the banana with a fork. Put the frosting in the bowl; mix up the banana and the frosting.

2. Spread the frosting on the bagels. Sprinkle the peanuts on the frosting.

6 servings

CARAMEL APPLE BAGELS

Slice up an apple (peel it first if you want to). Put the apple slices on a bagel. Put 8 caramel candies in a small pan; cook the candies on low heat until they melt. Stir them all the time. Pour the caramel over the apples. Sprinkle with chopped nuts if you want to!

Partytime Is Bageltime!

People throw parties for many different reasons. And the parties they throw reflect their diverse motives.

Our bachelor friend Seymour gives a birthday party for himself every time he meets a girl he'd like to get to know better. Sometimes he gives himself two birthday parties a month. Frankly, wearing those silly party hats with the elastic bands and eating the same licorice-flavored (Seymour's favorite) ice cream and cake every time isn't that much fun. But we always attend these parties because Seymour throws them just so he can play a game he invented called "Spin the Bagel." He explains to all his guests that this game improves on old-fashioned "Spin the Bottle" by relieving the uncertainty: Since nobody can ever figure out who the bagel is pointing at, everybody gets to kiss whomever they want!

The parties our friend Martha throws are much less intimate. In fact, they're more like recitals. Martha, you see, has always wanted to break into show business. But she can't interest anyone in booking her act. Plenty of nightclub owners invite her to audition when she phones and tells them the act is called "Martha Shambles and Her High-Flying Chicks." But after the audition, when they're left with all those feathers and corn kernels on stage, none of them calls back. So Martha only performs at her own parties. Actually, we aren't all that interested in the flock of chickens Martha has trained to fly on command, either. But Martha serves the best bagelette hors d'oeuvres we've ever tasted. She's quite talented in that department!

Our motives for party giving are rather simple: We look forward to having a good time. And we seize any opportunity to show off bagels in festive attire. Indeed, some of our best parties have been a "Come As You Are and Eat Bagels Bash" and a "Ring in the New Year and Bring Out the Bagels Gala Event." But whatever occasion prompts your invitations, you'll find that a Bagel Lancer Centerpiece or Pizzas with Pizzazz will "round out" the fun!

"I think Harvey just waits for us to arrive."

BAGEL LANCER CENTERPIECE

18 bagelettes (assorted flavors), toasted
1 package (8 ounces) cream cheese,
   room temperature
8 ounces liverwurst
3 slices American or Cheddar cheese, cut
   into fourths
3 slices Swiss cheese, cut into fourths
3 slices chicken or turkey loaf, cut into
   fourths
12 slices Italian salami

3 slices bologna, cut into fourths
2 ounces sliced corned beef
12 slices German salami
18 thin, small slices tomato
   Lettuce leaves
1 large red or green head cabbage
   Garnishes: Spanish olives, sweet
      and dill pickle chunks, cherry
      tomatoes, radish roses, cocktail
      onions

1. Spread top halves of bagelettes with cream cheese, bottom halves with
   liverwurst. Make sandwiches using remaining ingredients except the
   cabbage and garnishes.

2. Cut bottom third off cabbage. Place cabbage on serving plate. Stick 12
   bamboo skewers firmly into cabbage, spacing them evenly. Place
   sandwiches on skewers, placing 2 sandwiches on some skewers. Cut
   ends of skewers off with scissors if they are too long. Stick desired
   garnishes into cabbage with toothpicks. Allow guests to serve
   themselves.

12 servings

PIZZAS WITH PIZZAZZ!

1 cup chopped onion
1 clove garlic, minced
2 tablespoons olive oil
1 can (16 ounces) tomatoes, undrained
2 tablespoons tomato paste
¼ cup grated Parmesan cheese
½ teaspoon dried oregano leaves
¼ teaspoon dried basil leaves
¼ teaspoon fennel seeds, crushed
2 tablespoons minced parsley
1 pound Italian sausage, casing removed

½ pound sliced pepperoni or salami
1 cup chopped onion
1 cup chopped green pepper
1 cup sliced fresh mushrooms
  Butter or margarine
¼ cup sliced olives
  Anchovies, drained
4 ounces shredded Mozzarella cheese
4 ounces shredded Cheddar cheese
6 bagels, toasted

1. Saute 1 cup onion and the garlic in oil in large skillet until onion is tender, about 5 minutes. Stir in tomatoes and liquid, tomato paste, Parmesan cheese, oregano, basil and fennel. Heat to boiling; simmer uncovered until sauce has thickened, about 15 minutes. Stir in parsley.

2. Cook sausage over medium heat in small skillet until brown, about 5 minutes; drain. Saute pepperoni, 1 cup onion, the green pepper and mushrooms separately in butter. Place sausage, pepperoni, onion, green pepper, mushrooms, olives, anchovies and cheeses in separate small bowls.

3. Heat oven to 450°F. Place bagels, cut-sides up, on ungreased 16-inch pizza pan. Spread tomato sauce on bagels. Allow guests to sprinkle desired toppings on bagels. Bake uncovered until hot, about 10 minutes.

6 servings

PARTY PÂTÉ

1 pound chicken livers
1 small onion, minced
3 tablespoons butter or margarine
1 teaspoon poultry seasoning
1 teaspoon salt
¼ teaspoon white pepper
2 tablespoons brandy

1 cup whipping cream
    Pimiento strips
⅓ cup butter or margarine, room
    temperature
1 tablespoon brandy
12 bagelettes

1. Saute livers and onion in 3 tablespoons butter in large skillet until livers are cooked, but still slightly pink in the center, about 8 minutes. Stir in poultry seasoning, salt and pepper. Pour in 2 tablespoons brandy; flame. Remove skillet from heat; shake until flames are extinguished. Process liver mixture in blender or food processor until smooth; cool to room temperature.

2. Beat cream in small mixer bowl until stiff peaks form; fold into liver mixture. Pack liver mixture into 1-quart terrine or serving dish; decorate top with pimiento. Refrigerate loosely covered until firm, about 4 hours.

3. Beat ⅓ cup butter in small mixer bowl until fluffy. Gradually beat in 1 tablespoon brandy. Spread butter mixture on bagelettes, broil until brown, about 1 minute. Serve bagelettes with pâté.

12 servings

BAGEL NOTE: If you wish to unmold the pâté, line the terrine with plastic wrap before filling it with the liver mixture. Decorate with pimiento after unmolding.

SWEET 'N SOUR MEATBALLS

1 bagel, cut into 1-inch pieces
1 pound ground beef
2 eggs
1 small onion, finely chopped
¼ cup beer
½ teaspoon salt
  Pinch nutmeg

1½ cups beer
⅓ cup chutney
¼ cup catsup
¼ cup packed brown sugar
1 tablespoon soy sauce
1 tablespoon spicy brown mustard

1. Process bagel pieces in blender or food processor to make fine crumbs. Combine crumbs, beef, eggs, onion, ¼ cup beer, the salt and nutmeg in medium bowl. Shape meat mixture into 1-inch meatballs; place on ungreased cookie sheet. Broil 4 inches from heat source until brown, about 4 minutes on each side. Drain.

2. Combine remaining ingredients in large skillet; heat to boiling. Stir meatballs into sauce; simmer uncovered until meatballs are done and sauce thickened, 10 to 15 minutes. Serve in chafing dish.

12 appetizer servings

COCKTAIL BURGERS

1 pound ground beef
1 tablespoon Worcestershire sauce
1 tablespoon instant beef bouillon
1 teaspoon onion salt
1 teaspoon garlic powder
½ teaspoon pepper
12 bagelettes
12 cherry tomatoes, cut in half
2 tablespoons drained capers

1. Mix ground beef, Worcestershire sauce, bouillon, onion salt, garlic powder and pepper; spread mixture on bagelettes. Broil on cookie sheet 4-inches from heat source until meat is brown, 3 to 4 minutes.

2. Garnish each bagelette with cherry tomato half and capers.

24 appetizers

CAESAR'S SALAD BOWL

3 bagels *(garlic),* cut into ½-inch pieces
¾ cup butter or margarine
2 tablespoons olive oil
1 clove garlic, cut in half
8 cups romaine, cut into bite-size pieces
¼ cup olive or vegetable oil
1 tablespoon lemon juice
¼ teaspoon salt
6 grinds black pepper
¼ teaspoon Worcestershire sauce
½ teaspoon Dijon-style mustard
1 egg
¼ cup grated Parmesan cheese
6 anchovy fillets, cut in half

1. Saute bagel pieces in butter and 2 tablespoons olive oil in medium skillet until golden on all sides, about 5 minutes. Cool.

2. Rub salad bowl with cut sides of garlic. Arrange salad greens in bowl. Measure ¼ cup olive oil, the lemon juice, salt, pepper, Worcestershire sauce and mustard over greens; toss lightly several times. Break egg into a cup; slide onto salad. Toss until greens are evenly coated. Add Parmesan cheese, anchovies and toasted bagel pieces; toss to combine. Serve immediately.

4 to 6 servings

BAGEL NOTE: Assorted sliced meats can be served with the salad for a complete midnight supper. Bagel Bavarian (page 88) would be a delicious finale.

HOT-TIME CHILI

6 slices bacon
½ pound hot Italian sausage, casing
    removed
1 pound ground beef
2 green peppers, sliced
1 large onion, chopped
2 cloves garlic, minced
2 cans (16 ounces each) tomatoes,
    undrained
1 can (16 ounces) tomato sauce
1 can (15 ounces) kidney beans,
    drained
1 can (16 ounces) garbanzo beans,
    drained
2 to 3 teaspoons chili powder
1 teaspoon dried oregano leaves
½ teaspoon salt
¼ to ½ teaspoon crushed red pepper
¼ cup butter or margarine
1 clove garlic, minced
½ teaspoon chili powder
8 bagels

1. Fry bacon in Dutch oven until crisp. Remove bacon; drain and crumble.
   Cook sausage and ground beef in bacon drippings over medium heat
   until brown, about 8 minutes, stirring occasionally. Add peppers, onion
   and 2 cloves garlic; cook 5 minutes. Stir in tomatoes and liquid, tomato
   sauce, kidney beans, garbanzo beans, 2 to 3 teaspoons chili powder, the
   oregano, salt and red pepper. Simmer uncovered 1 hour.

2. Mix butter, 1 clove garlic and ½ teaspoon chili powder; spread on bagels.
   Broil 4 inches from heat source until brown, about 1 minute.

3. Ladle soup from crock; serve with bagels.

8 servings

CAVIAR CROWNS

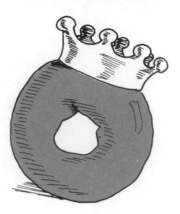

1 package (8 ounces) cream cheese,
    room temperature
⅓ cup mayonnaise or salad dressing
2 tablespoons drained capers
2 tablespoons minced parsley
1 tablespoon chopped chives
    Dash red pepper sauce
12 bagelettes
1 jar (4 ounces) red or black caviar
2 hard-cooked egg yolks

1. Beat cream cheese and mayonnaise in small mixer bowl until fluffy. Mix in capers, parsley, chives and red pepper sauce. Spread mixture on bagelettes.

2. Spoon about ½ teaspoon caviar in center of each bagelette. Press egg yolks through sieve; sprinkle over cream cheese and caviar.

24 appetizers

SNAZZY SARDINES

2 cans (4 ounces each) sardines, drained
¼ cup catsup
2 tablespoons chutney
2 teaspoons lemon juice
2 teaspoons Dijon-style mustard
1 teaspoon Worcestershire sauce
½ teaspoon onion salt
12 bagelettes, toasted
24 thin slices cucumber
    Parsley sprigs

1. Process sardines, catsup, chutney, lemon juice, mustard, Worcestershire sauce and onion salt in blender or food processor until smooth; spread on bagelettes. Place a slice of cucumber on each bagelette; garnish with parsley.

24 appetizers

ARTICHOKE PUFFS

1 can (8½ ounces) artichoke hearts, drained
12 bagelettes
¾ cup mayonnaise or salad dressing

¾ cup grated Parmesan cheese
1½ teaspoons prepared mustard
¼ teaspoon pepper

1. Heat oven to 450° F. Cut artichokes into quarters to make 24 pieces; place 1 piece on each bagelette half. Mix mayonnaise, Parmesan cheese, mustard and pepper; spoon mixture over artichokes.

2. Bake on ungreased cookie sheet until tops are puffed and golden, about 8 minutes. Let cool 5 minutes before serving.

24 appetizers

BLUE CHEESE BITES

1 package (3 ounces) cream cheese, room temperature
¼ cup butter or margarine, room temperature
1½ ounces blue cheese

1 tablespoon chopped chives
⅛ teaspoon white pepper
12 bagelettes, toasted
12 medium fresh mushrooms, sliced
Minced parsley

1. Beat cream cheese and butter in small mixer bowl until fluffy. Mix in blue cheese, chives and pepper.

2. Spread cheese mixture on bagelettes halves; top with sliced mushrooms. Garnish with parsley.

24 appetizers

SPINACH SOUFFLETTES

⅓ cup mayonnaise or salad dressing
12 bagelettes
1 package (12 ounces) frozen spinach souffle

1. Heat oven to 425° F. Spread mayonnaise on bagelette halves. Cut souffle into 12 pieces; cut each piece in half. Place 1 piece souffle on each bagelette.

2. Bake on ungreased cookie sheet until tops are puffed and golden, 30 to 35 minutes. Let cool 5 minutes before serving.

24 appetizers

Artsy-Craftsy Bagels

We've always admired people who could create works of art from paints, clay, metal and fabrics. But we've never been able to do so ourselves. Once we proudly made an ashtray that resembled a moon crater, but that was when we were younger. More recently, we sewed some curtains that looked all right after we hung the curtain rod at an angle. Most of our creative endeavors, however, have had to be donated to organizations charitable enough to take them.

So we were overjoyed to discover bagel crafts. They don't require a lot of know-how. And the creative inspiration comes with every glossy, smiling ring. For every bagel, you see, does have a "smile"—if you view the hole in the middle as a mouth and paint eyes above it and either paint or glue on some hair. In fact, every bagel—and to a more obvious degree every bagelette—has a different expression on its face, depending on whether the hole is wide with surprise, or scrunched into a smirk, or even slightly askew. If you paint on eyes, nose, lipstick, dimples, freckles and other features with food coloring, you can design a bagel work of art that's also completely edible. To turn your bagel into a necklace, greeting card, puppet head or Christmas tree ornament, or to form any kind of permanent friendship with it, you have to harden it first with a non-toxic acrylic polymer finish.

But a bagel is not just another pretty face. It can also be a candle holder or a napkin ring. Or a window-shade pull. Or a wristwatch—if you don't mind having time stand still. Several bagels can be turned into a cream cheese container, a trivet or a useless-but-highly-decorative kitchen wall-hanging. The sky's the limit with bagel crafts—even if you're an inveterate butterfingers like us.

On the following pages you'll find instructions for hardening and painting the bagels as well as suggestions for using the craft to set the theme for a Bagel Birthday Party and a Bageltime Brunch.

"I call it 'The View from Pacific Palisades at Sunset.'"

The Fine Art of Bagels

EDIBLE BAGEL ART

There are times when you want to paint your bagel and eat it too. For example, you might want to paint the names of dinner guests on bagels and then let them eat their "place cards." For such purposes, rub the surface of the bagel lightly with a vegetable brush; this will allow food coloring to adhere smoothly. Then paint on names, as well as faces and messages if desired, with a small paint brush dipped in food coloring.

PERMANENT BAGEL ART

If you secretly long to see your bagel art hung in a museum—or on a Christmas tree at least—you have to let the bagels get stale and dry and then finish them with acrylic polymer emulsion. The polymer also serves as a glue; so you can apply it to harden the bagel and use it to affix hooks, hairpins, wooden sticks or other adjuncts at the same time. Polymer-finished bagels are non-toxic; so if your dog chews up your bagel necklace or ornament, he'll be all right even if your masterpiece isn't. Here are general instructions for permanent bagel art:

Materials needed: Bagels or bagelettes; non-toxic acrylic polymer emulsion (available at artists' supply or craft shops); small and medium paint brushes; non-toxic opaque water colors; hair pins, ornament hooks or wooden ice cream sticks (see specific crafts for items needed).

1. Let bagel halves stand uncovered at room temperature until stale and very hard, 2 to 3 days.

2. Lay bagels on newspaper; paint cut surfaces with acrylic polymer emulsion. If appropriate, position a hair pin, wooden stick or other item on 1 bagel half; place second bagel half on top. Press bagel halves together. Let stand until dry, about 1 hour. Paint 1 outer surface of bagel with polymer; let stand until dry, about 1 hour. Repeat with second outer surface. (If hooks have been inserted into bagels, you can attach strings to the hooks and hang the bagels from a coat hanger. Then you can paint the entire outside of the bagel with polymer at one time.)

3. Paint bagels with opaque water colors and decorate them according to directions for specific crafts. Opaque water colors will dry with a dull finish; for a shiny finish, mix the paint with several drops of acrylic polymer emulsion.

120

BAGEL GREETINGS

To make a bagel greeting card, brush the cut surface of a bagelette half with acrylic polymer emulsion. Position the bagelette half, cut-side down, on a piece of poster board that will fit into a large envelope. Brush the outer surface of the bagelette with polymer and let it dry. Paint the name of the recipient and his or her face on the bagelette. Use poster paints or felt-tip pens to write a message on the card. Some appropriate messages:

Valentine's Day—"Won't You Be My Bagelhead?"
Graduation—"You Finally Made It, You Bagelhead!"
Birth Announcement—"It's a Bagel!"
Anniversary—"All Best Bagels!"
Birthday—"Happy Bagelday!"
All Occasions—"Love and Bagels!"

We're sure you can do better than that! But you get the message. . . .

BAGEL BAUBLES

Everybody likes to wear bagelette necklaces. Some men like to have them dangling across their sexy chests; others use them to anchor their neckties. Some women enjoy wearing bagelettes that announce "Hi! I'm Gladys" (or whatever is appropriate); others prefer anonymous flowers or designs on their jewelry. Whatever your style, you can create a necklace by brushing two halves of a bagelette with acrylic polymer emulsion and pressing a hair pin between the halves so that the top of the pin forms a loop for a chain or ribbon. Then brush the outer surfaces of the bagelette with polymer and allow them to dry. Paint your bagelette with opaque water colors and insert a chain, shoelace or ribbon through the loop.

MERRY BAGELS

To decorate a Christmas tree, you can make Santa Claus or angel ornaments by following the instructions for making bagelette necklaces. Decorate the ornaments by affixing bits of cotton (for beards), yarn, felt and ribbon, as well as sequins or beads, with school glue. To create a "portrait" tree ornament for every member of your family, trim a small snapshot of each person so that it will fit inside a bagel and the face will be visible through the bagel hole. Brush the cut surfaces of two regular bagel halves (not bagelettes) with acrylic polymer emulsion. Press the photo face-down on one bagel half and position a hair pin for a hook. Press the bagel halves together and proceed as for other ornaments. (Or close the bagel, let it harden, and hammer a nail with a large head into the top of the bagel; then tie a string around the nail and tap the nail to secure the string.)

121

Bagel Birthday Party

Bagels belong at birthday parties. They're festive, fun to eat—and sometimes downright silly. So we've planned this occasion for kids, although not a few of our adult friends also get a kick out of playing "Pin the Bagel on the Clown." You can use as many of these ideas as you wish to set the bagel theme:

BAGEL BANQUET

Paint each guest's name on a bagel with food coloring and use the bagels for place cards. (You can split the bagels and spread the halves with butter or cream cheese before putting them back together and painting the tops.) Then set out platters of cold cuts, cheese, carrot and celery curls, olive and radish halves and leaf lettuce, along with boxes of toothpicks. Let the kids turn their bagels into whatever creations they find most tantalizing—with lettuce "hair," olive "eyes," bologna "bodies," etc.—before they eat them.

BAGEL PUPPETS

Make a mini-puppet party favor for each guest by finishing bagelettes with acrylic polymer emulsion and inserting a wooden ice cream pop stick between the two halves. Paint a face on the hardened bagelette. Sew a fabric sleeve for each puppet and gather the top to fit the base of the bagelette. Glue the top of the sleeve to the bagelette. Decorate the puppet head with yarn hair, a felt hat or whatever fits the character. The kids can put on a puppet show during the party by moving the puppet heads with the attached wooden sticks. Then they can take home the puppets as souvenirs.

PIN THE BAGEL ON THE CLOWN

Use a large piece of felt as the background for the clown's face. Cut out all the clown's features—a circle for the face, red cheeks, big eyes, a grinning mouth, hat, bow tie, etc.—from felt and glue them to the background. Leave a space where the nose should be and tack the clown to the wall (or you can glue the felt background to a dowel rod and hang the clown with picture wire). Glue two ½-inch-wide strips of Velcro fabric fastener to the cut surface of a bagel half. Blindfold the kids and let them try to stick the nose on the clown.

OTHER BAGEL GAMES

Divide the kids into teams and let them run a relay race with bagels on their heads; the team that deposits the most bagels in a bucket without dropping them gets a prize. Or play "Huckle Buckle Bagel" by hiding a bagelette (in plain sight) and asking the kids to try and find it. Bagelhead® necklaces make dandy prizes for winners and losers alike!

Bageltime Brunch

Not only are bagels the most delicious food you can serve for brunch, but they're also the most decorative! Here are some ways to make bageleaters feel welcome:

BAGEL RINGS

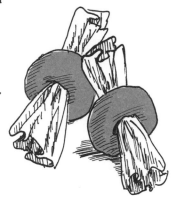

Harden and paint a set of assorted regular-size bagels to use as napkin rings. You can re-use the rings for many brunches or paint guests' names on them and let them double as place cards. You can also make cheery, personalized place cards by following the technique used for "Bagel Greetings."

BAGEL BOXES

Make individual cream cheese holders from bagelettes. You need 2½ bagelettes, cut in half, for each box. One half is the bottom; the other four halves form the sides. Attach the sides to the bottom with toothpicks. You can let the boxes get stale—they will become hard and sturdy. Or serve them fresh and let guests eat them. Either way, place a small paper muffin cup in each bagel box and fill it with a scoop of cream cheese. For party appeal, color the cream cheese before you scoop it by beating it in a blender or with a hand mixer with chopped pimientos, chopped black olives, minced purple or green onions, dill, crushed pineapple or minced lox.

BAGEL TOWERS

A ⅜-inch dowel rod glued with school glue into the hole of a bagel will make a handsome holder for a half dozen bagels.

FLICKERING BAGELS

When the occasion calls for candlelight, you can make a wreath of bagels to hold as many romantic tapers as you wish. Tie the bagels together with ribbons and insert a thin candle into each bagel. Be careful not to let the tapers burn down too far!

BAGEL TALK:
An Annotated "Glossyring" of Common Terms

BAGEL   A round chewy roll with a hole in the middle—but only if you insist on literal definitions. In fact, "bagel" means different things to different people; it may mean nourishment, solace, challenge or reward, depending on your point of view. Also, tone of voice can indicate fluctuation in meaning. When someone yells at you, "Take your fingers out of my cream cheese, you bagel!" it is not the same thing as when a rock singer croons, "Plee-eze be my bagel to-ni-iight."

BAGELEATER   One of millions of satisfied chompers, no two of whom are exactly alike. While all bageleaters share a fondness for bagels, their reasons differ, as do their modes of BAGELEATING. Among famous bageleaters, Charles H. "Iron Jaws" Stropper has captured top honors for attacking the tallest stack of bagels (17) in one bite; Millicent Teacosy has been awarded a certificate of devoted service for her valiant efforts to save the souls of English muffin devotees; and Ellsworth Farnsworth has been cited numerous times for his groundbreaking dissertation, "Wherein It Is Proved that the Sum of the Parts is Always Greater than the Circumference of the Hole."

BAGELEATING   For some people it's a hobby, for others a love affair. For our friend Gloria, it's a mode of consuming food in bed that produces fewer crumbs than any other she's found. For Max Chewitz, known in the neighborhood as "Hungry Max," it's a business: "Thirty years ago a bagel baker hired me to sit in his window and savor the product. I did such a good job that business grew by leaps and bagels. They couldn't pass the bakery without stopping to buy. I discovered I had a special knack for chewing with gusto in public. So I found my calling and I've been here ever since."

BAGELETTE   A chubby miniature that's so cute you don't know whether to eat it or turn it into a BAGELHEAD® necklace.

BAGELHEAD   An artform created by Willie Evans of New Haven, Connecticut, who ranks with Grandma Moses among the great naive American artists. Willie is so naive that the first time he saw a bagelette he thought it was making eyes at him. And smiling. And being friendly. So he painted a face on it. Then he tied a shoelace to it and started wearing it around his neck. Pretty soon, everyone else wanted a bagelette necklace too. So after years of being involved with various enterprises, Willie won fame and affection (if not fortune) by creating Bagelheads, which have come to be known as "the food you love to wear."

BEPP   An acronym that stands for Bageleater's Personality Profile, a test devised by the brilliant psychoanalyst Dr. Sigmund Lox to diagnose the flavor preferences of bageleaters. After years of treating unhappy patients with other methods, Dr. Lox hit upon a specialized form of therapy that has proved 300 percent effective (this figure reflects the fact that each patient has leaked the secret to an average of two friends). On the first visit, Dr. Lox checks the patient's dental record and administers the simple test. Sample test questions include: "Do you see spots before your eyes that look like raisins?"; "Do you sometimes fall asleep at night drooling over onions?"; "Do you dream of the day when you can eat all the garlic you want?"; "Do you consider yourself a 'good egg'?" The answers are very revealing of patients' innermost cravings. After scoring the test, Dr. Lox knows exactly what kind of bagels to bring to the next session. The patients keep coming back for more; they claim that no other doctor has so much sensitivity to the true nature of their desires.

BIALY   The only half-breed allowed into the company of bagels. But it doesn't grip your teeth the way a true bagel does. And instead of a cheery hole in the center, a bialy has only a depression.

BRUNCH   A breakfast that gets off to a late start and lasts until everybody feels like taking a nap. Or, alternatively, a lunch that gets off to an early start and lasts until nobody's hungry for dinner.

CREAM CHEESE   Originally, a featherbed for LOX. Now commonly used in connection with everything from bagelette hors d'oeuvres to bagel cheesecake.

DOUGHNUT   Part of various disparaging terms used to describe a bagel, such as "a petrified doughnut" and "a doughnut with rigor mortis." Needless to say, we don't use that kind of language around here.

FRESSER   Not to be confused with "freezer," which is where bagels are kept, a fresser is someone who has mastered the two-fisted method of bagel consumption. Which is to say, he eats them two at a time. Maybe one with salami and mustard, the other with chopped liver.

HOLE   A hole is to a bagel what a punch line is to a joke; i.e., if it doesn't have one, it doesn't qualify. Which fact has prompted one bagel baker with a philosophical bent to write a treatise titled "Sometimes Nothing is Just as Important as Something."

LOX   In Germany, salmon is called "lox" (spelled *lachs*). In this country, succulent, salty, sliced smoked salmon is called "lox" for short. It's no wonder! Would you go into a store and ask for a quarter pound of "succulent, salty, sliced smoked salmon"?

MAVEN   A connoisseur; someone who not only knows his bagels from his lox but also knows his lox from his NOVA.

NATURAL   Used variously to mean "not phony" or "without artificial additives." Bagels qualify as natural on both counts.

NOSHER   A person who leads the fullest possible existence—full of bagels, full of chopped liver, full of cheese, full of sardines—full of whatever he can get his hands on on those frequent occasions when vague yearnings stir within him.

NOVA   This is a form of lox that's not really lox and that does not, as its name might imply, come from Nova Scotia. Therefore, it is an esoteric food, to say the least, and one much prized by mavens, who claim it's provender fit for the gods. Why such fancy praise? Because while nova is much less salty than brine-cured lox, it is nevertheless a form of smoked salmon eminently well suited to bagels. Did you ever hear of anyone asking for Scottish or Irish smoked salmon on a bagel?

TAM   A Yiddish term meaning "taste" or "flavor" (and pronounced "tom") that should become more widely adopted into American parlance. In fact, we'd like to mount a campaign toward that end for several reasons. First, because "tam" can be used more emphatically than "flavor"; for example, you can say "This bagel and pastrami sandwich has real *tam*!" and convey a sense of pleasure that "flavor" never could capture. Secondly, "tam" can be applied to people as well as to food. So if you see a man pull out a snack of bagels and cheese to eat on the bus, for example, you can say admiringly, "That guy has real tam!" Furthermore, "tam" can express universal camaraderie unlike any other term: When you see a little old lady in her proverbial tennis sneakers sitting in the park and unwrapping her lunch of kiwi marmalade and bagelettes, you should be able to strike up a conversation by saying, "Lady, you have real tam!" And if she does have real tam, she won't strike back!

TEETHING   The critical stage of human development at which an infant is introduced to the solace of a bagel when he or she needs it most.

RECIPE INDEX